AVA PICKETT

Ava Pickett is from Clacton-on-Sea. She is a writer for stage and screen. Her screen work includes shows such as *Brassic*, *The Great*, *Bad Education* and *How to Get to Heaven from Belfast*. *1536* was originally commissioned by the Almeida Theatre as part of their Genesis Almeida New Playwrights, Big Plays Programme. It won the Susan Smith Blackburn Award and received a special commendation from the George Devine Award. *1536* is Ava Pickett's debut play.

Other Titles in this Series

Waleed Akhtar
THE ART OF ILLUSION *after* Alexis Michalik
KABUL GOES POP: MUSIC TELEVISION AFGHANISTAN
THE P WORD
THE REAL ONES

Chris Bush
THE ASSASSINATION OF KATIE HOPKINS
    with Matt Winkworth
THE CHANGING ROOM
CHRIS BUSH PLAYS: ONE
A DOLL'S HOUSE *after* Ibsen
FAUSTUS: THAT DAMNED WOMAN
HUNGRY
JANE EYRE *after* Brontë
THE LAST NOËL
OTHERLAND
ROBIN HOOD AND THE CHRISTMAS HEIST
    with Matt Winkworth
ROCK / PAPER / SCISSORS
STANDING AT THE SKY'S EDGE
    with Richard Hawley
STEEL

Jez Butterworth
THE FERRYMAN
THE HILLS OF CALIFORNIA
JERUSALEM
JEZ BUTTERWORTH PLAYS: ONE
JEZ BUTTERWORTH PLAYS: TWO
MOJO
THE NIGHT HERON
PARLOUR SONG
THE RIVER
THE WINTERLING

Caryl Churchill
BLUE HEART
CHURCHILL PLAYS: THREE
CHURCHILL PLAYS: FOUR
CHURCHILL PLAYS: FIVE
CHURCHILL: SHORTS
CLOUD NINE
DING DONG THE WICKED
A DREAM PLAY *after* Strindberg
DRUNK ENOUGH TO SAY I LOVE YOU?
ESCAPED ALONE
FAR AWAY
GLASS. KILL. BLUEBEARD'S FRIENDS. IMP.
HERE WE GO
HOTEL
ICECREAM
LIGHT SHINING IN BUCKINGHAMSHIRE
LOVE AND INFORMATION
MAD FOREST
A NUMBER
PIGS AND DOGS
SEVEN JEWISH CHILDREN
THE SKRIKER
THIS IS A CHAIR
THYESTES *after* Seneca
TRAPS
WHAT IF IF ONLY

Branden Jacobs-Jenkins
APPROPRIATE
THE COMEUPPANCE
GLORIA
AN OCTOROON

Lucy Kirkwood
BEAUTY AND THE BEAST
    with Katie Mitchell
BLOODY WIMMIN
THE CHILDREN
CHIMERICA
HEDDA *after* Ibsen
THE HUMAN BODY
IT FELT EMPTY WHEN THE HEART WENT AT FIRST BUT IT IS ALRIGHT NOW
LUCY KIRKWOOD PLAYS: ONE
MOSQUITOES
NSFW
RAPTURE
TINDERBOX
THE WELKIN

Benedict Lombe
LAVA
SHIFTERS

Winsome Pinnock
LEAVE TAKING
PIG HEART BOY *after* Malorie Blackman
ROCKETS AND BLUE LIGHTS
TAKEN
TITUBA

Jack Thorne
2ND MAY 1997
AFTER LIFE *after* Hirokazu Kore-eda
BUNNY
BURYING YOUR BROTHER IN THE PAVEMENT
A CHRISTMAS CAROL *after* Dickens
THE END OF HISTORY…
HOPE
JACK THORNE PLAYS: ONE
JACK THORNE PLAYS: TWO
JUNKYARD
LET THE RIGHT ONE IN
    after John Ajvide Lindqvist
THE MOTIVE AND THE CUE
MYDIDAE
THE SOLID LIFE OF SUGAR WATER
STACY & FANNY AND FAGGOT
WHEN WINSTON WENT TO WAR WITH THE WIRELESS
WHEN YOU CURE ME
WOYZECK *after* Büchner

debbie tucker green
BORN BAD
DEBBIE TUCKER GREEN PLAYS: ONE
DIRTY BUTTERFLY
EAR FOR EYE
HANG
NUT
A PROFOUNDLY AFFECTIONATE, PASSIONATE DEVOTION TO SOMEONE (– *NOUN*)
RANDOM
STONING MARY
TRADE & GENERATIONS
TRUTH AND RECONCILIATION

Phoebe Waller-Bridge
FLEABAG

Ross Willis
WOLFIE
WONDER BOY

Ava Pickett

1536

NICK HERN BOOKS
London
www.nickhernbooks.co.uk

A Nick Hern Book

1536 first published in Great Britain in 2025 as a paperback original by Nick Hern Books Limited, The Glasshouse, 49a Goldhawk Road, London W12 8QP

1536 copyright © 2025 Ava Pickett

Ava Pickett has asserted her right to be identified as the author of this work

Front cover: photography by Felicity McCabe; art direction by Studio Doug

Designed and typeset by Nick Hern Books, London
Printed in Great Britain by Mimeo Ltd, Huntingdon, Cambridgeshire PE29 6XX

A CIP catalogue record for this book is available from the British Library

ISBN 978 1 83904 420 5

CAUTION   All rights whatsoever in this play are strictly reserved. Requests to reproduce the text in whole or in part should be addressed to the publisher. This book may not be used, in whole or in part, for the development or training of artificial intelligence technologies or systems.

Amateur Performing Rights   Applications for performance, including readings and excerpts, by amateurs in the English language throughout the world should be addressed to the Performing Rights Manager, Nick Hern Books, The Glasshouse, 49a Goldhawk Road, London W12 8QP, *tel* +44 (0)20 8749 4953, *email* rights@nickhernbooks.co.uk, except as follows:

Australia: ORiGiN Theatrical, *email* enquiries@originmusic.com.au, *web* www.origintheatrical.com.au

New Zealand: Play Bureau, 20 Rua Street, Mangapapa, Gisborne, 4010, *tel* +64 21 258 3998, *email* info@playbureau.com

United States of America and Canada: Curtis Brown Ltd, see details below.

Professional Performing Rights   Application for performance by professionals in any medium and in any language throughout the world should be addressed to Curtis Brown Ltd, Cunard House, 15 Regent Street, St James's, London SW1Y 4LR, *tel* +44 (0)20 7393 4400, *fax* +44 (0)20 7393 4401, *email* cb@curtisbrown.co.uk

No performance of any kind may be given unless a licence has been obtained. Applications should be made before rehearsals begin. Publication of this play does not necessarily indicate its availability for amateur performance.

www.nickhernbooks.co.uk/environmental-policy

Nick Hern Books' authorised representative in the EU is
Easy Access System Europe – Mustamäe tee 50, 10621 Tallinn, Estonia
email gpsr.requests@easproject.com

1536 was first performed at the Almeida Theatre, London, on 6 May 2025, with the following cast:

WILLIAM	Angus Cooper
JANE	Liv Hill
RICHARD	Adam Hugill
ANNA	Siena Kelly
MARIELLA	Tanya Reynolds

Director	Lyndsey Turner
Designer	Max Jones
Lighting Designer	Jack Knowles
Lighting Design Concept developed with	Tim Lutkin
Sound Designer	Tingying Dong
Composer and Arranger	Will Stuart
Movement and Intimacy Director	Anna Morrissey
Casting Director	Amy Ball CDG
Fight Director	Sam Lyon-Behan
Dialect Coach	Edda Sharpe
Costume Supervisor	Sabia Smith
Assistant Director	Taiwo Ava Oyebola
Almeida Makers Design Placement	Bolu Dairo

Special Thanks to:

Emily, Phoebe and Madeleine.

You read this play in cafés and rehearsal rooms and foyers, over and over again, accepting pints as payment and offering endless support. I'm too embarrassed to say it to your faces so I'll put it in writing: I love you, thank you.

And obviously to my mum, Alex, who sat at a parents' evening in Year Eleven and went, 'Well, why not give the dream a go?' I love you, thank you.

A.P.

In memory of the blisteringly wonderful Sarah Davey-Hull, without her limitless encouragement, generosity and talent, this play may have never quite got out into the world and she is deeply missed and constantly felt.

Characters

ANNA, *twenty-three, in service*
MARIELLA, *twenty-two, midwife*
JANE, *nineteen, a wife*

RICHARD, *twenty-five, a man with power*
WILLIAM, *twenty-nine, a man with power*

Everyone is from Essex.

Note on Text

Punctuation (or lack of) is used to indicate pace, rhythm and tone.

A forward slash (/) indicates when the next line comes in.

Do it fast.

Do it simply.

This text went to press before the end of rehearsals and so may differ slightly from the play as performed.

Scene One

England. May, 1536. A field in Essex.

ANNA *fucks* RICHARD *fast up against a curled tree. It is sweaty, rushed, stolen.*

They finish and he steps away from her, she slides down the tree.

He pulls his trousers up as she pulls her skirts down. When done, they stop and look at each other, she laughs and he laughs too, shaking his head.

He steps forward, pushes her hair out of her face. She bites the inside of his wrist, he winces and laughs.

RICHARD. Here.

He hands her a turquoise bracelet.

For when I'm not with you.

She takes the bracelet. He stares at her and smiles. They kiss again, passionately, hungrily.

And then he goes. She watches him go and her smile fades, like smoke disappearing into air.

Fuck.

Scene Two

England. May, 1536. The same field in Essex. It is hot. It is bright.

Now ANNA*'s body lies on her front in the field. Unmoving. Spread out, skirts hitched up, soaking up the sun. She looks dead.*

There is a breeze. There is a bird. Somewhere else, men are arguing over a fence about a debt that has not been paid, about trust that has been broken, about a consequence that will come.

Suddenly, JANE *arrives, panting and sweating, and* ANNA *jolts up, surprised.*

JANE. Hi – hi hi – oh god – sorry –

ANNA. What's happened?

JANE. I – sorry I can't – I can't breathe – hang on –

ANNA. Jane, what's happened? Something good, something bad, what?

    JANE *nods feverishly, still panting.*

    What, something to you? Something to me? What? Speak! Tell me, quick! Quick!

JANE. It's, it's the King. He's –

ANNA. The King? The King's dead?! FUCK OFF is the King dead! No!

JANE. No, no, he's, he's not dead don't worry!

ANNA. Oh I'm not worried.

JANE. What?

ANNA. I said I'm *not* worried.

JANE. Oh.

    JANE *stops. Still breathing heavily, she swallows, thinking, processing. She looks back where she came from, then back at* ANNA.

SCENE TWO 11

What, if you – if I had come here and said the King's died you wouldn't be worried?

ANNA. Nah.

JANE. Not even a little bit?

ANNA. Not really.

JANE. But it's the King.

ANNA. I know he's the King.

JANE. and he'd be dead.

ANNA. yeah and?

JANE. and you wouldn't, what you wouldn't even be *slightly* worried, not even a bit?

ANNA. Nah, not really.

JANE. Anna he's the King of England.

ANNA. Yeah I'm aware of that.

JANE. and if he died there's no heir, he's not got like, a legitimate male heir it would be, it'd be chaos.

ANNA. Yeah alright.

JANE. Chaos – everywhere –

ANNA. Sure but look, like he's not, he's not, John is he?

Beat.

JANE. What?

ANNA. He's not *John* is he?

JANE. John who?

ANNA. Pollen.

JANE. John Pollen.

ANNA. Yeah. It wouldn't be like *him* dying would it? It's not like *him* dying is it?

JANE. John Pollen, the baker?

ANNA. Yep.

JANE. What you'd be worried if, if John Pollen, the baker, died?

ANNA. Yes.

JANE. What you'd be *more* worried if John Pollen the baker died instead of the King of England?

ANNA. Correct.

JANE. If he dropped dead right now?

ANNA. Sure.

JANE. Why?!

ANNA. Cos it affects me, John Pollen dying affects me directly!

JANE. The King dying affects you directly!

ANNA. Not really! I mean when has the King ever given me a free loaf? Or a bun? Or a roll?

JANE. Anna you can't be serious, it's the King!

ANNA. Alright what's his name then?

JANE. What?

ANNA. What's the King's name Jane? What's his name?

JANE. It's, it's, well it's, it's King.

ANNA. Yeah go on, what's the next bit? After the King bit. King what?

JANE *struggles,* ANNA *laughs.*

See! You don't even know!

JANE *laughs.*

JANE. No! I *do* know! I do know! I just! I've just forgotten for a second, for a moment!

ANNA. Alright well the moment's passed so what is it?!

JANE. Anna...

ANNA. Nope! Incorrect! That's me! Next!

JANE. Erm...

ANNA. Come on...

JANE. Henry! It's Henry! Ha!!

ANNA. Well done. But yeah I care more about John Pollen dying than the King of England if that's what you're asking, now do you want to know a secret?

JANE. Will I end up dead?

ANNA. What?

JANE. Is it a secret that will get me killed cos if it is, then no thanks. Not really.

ANNA. What secrets have I told you that have got you killed?

JANE. Well none.

ANNA. Exactly.

JANE. Yet!

> ANNA *reaches into her dress and pulls out the bracelet that* RICHARD *gave her. It stops* JANE *dead.*

Oh my god.

ANNA. I know.

JANE. *Anna.*

ANNA. I know.

JANE. That's like – that's like *jewels*.

ANNA. Yep.

JANE. Like *actual* jewels.

ANNA. Yep.

JANE. Like *proper* Jewels.

ANNA. Alright Jane, it's just a fucking bracelet.

JANE. Can I touch it?

ANNA. You *are* touching it.

JANE. But can I like, put it on?

ANNA. Sure, if it'll fit.

JANE *puts it on, examines herself.*

JANE. Who gave it to you?

ANNA. Can't say.

JANE. John Pollen?

ANNA. As if!

JANE. You just said you cared if he died!

ANNA. Oh my god! Cos I like free stuff Jane! And because it's boring to look at ugly men!

JANE. Thomas Cotley?

ANNA. Thomas Cotley? Fuck off would it be Thomas Cotley!

JANE. You said you'd throw yourself off a bridge for him last month.

ANNA. Oh shut up Jane no I didn't.

JANE. It's a big thing, to have jewels.

ANNA. You can keep it if you want.

JANE. Oh Anna, no I couldn't.

ANNA. It looks nice.

JANE. No…

ANNA. Makes you look interesting…

JANE. Anna I can't. I haven't got the wrists for it –

ANNA. Your wrists are fine!

JANE. They're not!

ANNA. Jane just accept the fucking bracelet!

Beat. ANNA *tries to be nice.* JANE *puts it on and is thrilled.*

See? Now people will wonder about you. They'll go who is Jane getting *bracelets* from? Who is Jane disappearing off to meet? They'll think you've got admirers, they'll think you're *mysterious.*

JANE. You said I didn't have the bone structure to be mysterious.

ANNA. Well you would if you ate less.

JANE. I thought your father said you weren't to accept gifts from boys any more.

ANNA. Urgh who cares.

JANE. He won't like it. He'll fight you on it

ANNA. Well he'll lose

JANE. but you won't win!

ANNA *stares at* JANE *sulkily, she's ruined it. Fuck Jane. Fuck dumb Jane.* ANNA *pulls at the grass.*

ANNA. Go on then.

JANE. What?

ANNA. Your news. You had news. You ran up here to tell me something –

JANE. Oh yeah –

ANNA. – Like a fucking dog.

Beat. ANNA *stares at* JANE, *her cheeks are red.* JANE *doesn't know what to do when* ANNA *gets like this.*

MARIELLA *(faint, offstage)*. OI!

Both JANE *and* ANNA *look to watch* MARIELLA *(offstage) approach.* ANNA *smiles, stands up and yells:*

ANNA. Hurry up! Jane's got news!

MARIELLA *(faint, offstage)*. What?!

ANNA. News! JANE'S GOT FUCKING NEWS.

MARIELLA, *sweating, carrying a basket, arrives and throws it on the ground.*

MARIELLA. Oh my fucking life, I am *so* hot.

ANNA. So hot.

JANE. So hot.

MARIELLA. It's not been this hot before has it?

JANE. I think maybe last May was this warm.

ANNA. No it wasn't it's far hotter this year. How'd you get away!?

MARIELLA *plops herself down on the grass next to* ANNA.

MARIELLA. I didn't. I'm hiding from Agnes. Anna put your stockings on, if a man comes…

ANNA. They'd think themselves lucky –

MARIELLA *is running a small bottle of water over some scissors.*

URGH MARIELLA DON'T DO THAT!

MARIELLA. I HAVE TO DO IT OR IT CRUSTS.

JANE. Why are you hiding from Agnes?

MARIELLA. We were meant to go up to Updale Hall today.

ANNA. Urgh hasn't Eleanor had the fucking kid yet?

MARIELLA. Nope.

ANNA. When?

MARIELLA. Maybe a month? Maybe more?

JANE. She must be so uncomfortable.

ANNA. Does she look awful? Is her neck swollen? I bet her neck's swollen.

MARIELLA. Why would her neck be swollen?

SCENE TWO 17

ANNA. That's what happens when you're pregnant.

MARIELLA. Incorrect.

JANE. Is she scared?

ANNA. Is she gonna die?!

JANE. Anna!

ANNA. What?! It's just a question!

JANE. That's sinful.

ANNA. Asking a question ain't sinful Jane what's sinful is the state of your fucking hair mate.

MARIELLA. I doubt Eleanor's gonna die, the amount of staff they've got.

ANNA. You know I had to serve them the other night? Her and William? They came up to have dinner with Aldward. Didn't say a *word* to each other, looked *miserable* as sin. He hates her you can tell.

MARIELLA. Thanks. I don't believe you but thanks.

ANNA. He does! She's so boring *and* she eats like a pig.

JANE. Well I feel sorry for Eleanor, she's probably terrified.

ANNA. Pregnancy's part of life Jane, we all have to do it.

MARIELLA. Alright well you've not done it yet.

ANNA. Yes but when I do, I definitely won't be terrified and I won't be swanning about doing nothing like Eleanor fucking Updale.

MARIELLA. You absolutely will! It's all you do now! Look at you!

ANNA. It's not my fault Aldward's away in London. You know I slept in their bed the other night?

JANE. No you didn't!

ANNA. The sheets were so heavy, I didn't wake up *once* it was like being under the earth! I had to! For my *tired* eyes!

JANE. He'll strike you if he finds out.

ANNA. No he won't he doesn't *believe* in striking his women.

JANE. So unfair!

MARIELLA. You've been in his favour ever since you helped him with that fever.

ANNA. Yeah well maybe Mariella he's grateful I helped him *escape death*!

MARIELLA. I taught you that remedy!

ANNA. Everyone knows a dried fish on the chest helps solve a fever, you can't take the credit.

MARIELLA. Unbelievable.

ANNA. Mariella you *could've* gone into service with me, you *chose* to be a midwife!

MARIELLA. No! My grandmother chose to be a midwife, I had no part in it and honestly it's fucking horrible, but I am very good at it.

JANE. You are very good at it.

ANNA. She is very good at it.

They all laugh.

Alright quick then before I have to go back. Jane had news.

JANE. I did? I did!

MARIELLA. What?! From where?

JANE. London.

ANNA. WHAT! You didn't say it was from London!

JANE. You were talking about the bracelet!

MARIELLA. Bracelet?! What bracelet?

ANNA. Jane, show her the bracelet.

JANE shows MARIELLA the bracelet and MARIELLA can't believe it.

MARIELLA. Fuck off… Anna…

ANNA. I know.

JANE. She won't say who gave it to her. It's *not* John Pollen – although he's been giving her free loaves.

MARIELLA. WHAT?

ANNA. Men like to give me gifts Mariella it's not my fault.

JANE. Was it George Hatchworth?

ANNA. George Hatchworth! As if!

MARIELLA. Mark Canning? Oh! Oh! Lewis Thorbold?!

JANE. OH! THE MAN IN THE MARKET WHO SAID YOU HAD EYES LIKE THE SKY?!

ANNA. No. Never. And oh my god, I forgot he'd said that!

MARIELLA. Wait, is it a proposal?

ANNA. Maybe.

MARIELLA. Anna! Is it?!

ANNA. You'll have to wait and see won't you?! A girl doesn't kiss and tell Mariella!

MARIELLA. Fuck off, yes you do! All you do is kiss and all you do is tell!

ANNA *laughs and smacks* MARIELLA *playfully*.

JANE. God it must be so amazing, to have secrets.

ANNA. You should get yourself some. Okay go on then quick Jane what is it?

JANE. What? Oh! Yes! Right so it's about the Queen!

ANNA. What? You said it was about the King?!

JANE. Well yes it's about the King but *really* it's about the Queen

ANNA. Is she pregnant?!

JANE. Nope.

MARIELLA. Idiot.

JANE. He's arrested her.

Beat. They all freeze. The air shifts.

ANNA. What?

Beat.

Arrested her? What d'you mean?

MARIELLA. What he's *had* her arrested?

JANE. Yeah.

ANNA. What he's ordered it? The King?

JANE. Yes!

ANNA. The Queen?

JANE. Yes yes Anne Boleyn arrested!

MARIELLA. But –

ANNA. But, she's the *Queen*.

MARIELLA. On what grounds?

JANE. I don't know. Father said, something about – about treason.

MARIELLA. What?! Treason?!

ANNA. No. No, you've got that, you've got that wrong you've, you've *heard* that wrong.

JANE. How can I hear the word 'queen' wrong?

ANNA. You mixed up bed and bread the other day.

JANE. Nothing rhymes with queen, Anna.

ANNA. Spleen does. Mean does.

JANE. I didn't hear it wrong, she's been arrested and she's in the Tower.

MARIELLA. The *Tower*? He's put her in the fucking Tower?

ANNA. Alright when then? When did this happen?

JANE. It happened the day Father left London so, I dunno, maybe two days ago.

ANNA. *Two* days ago?! Oh! Well she's probably already out then! If it was two days ago, it's probably already finished!

JANE. Do you think so?

ANNA. Of course it is! She's the fucking Queen, Jane! Since when have you known a queen to get arrested? I mean this is, this is old news, tired news. Right?

MARIELLA. Right.

A pause, they all contemplate this.

ANNA. I mean I just thought you were gonna say something about the chickens.

JANE. You think I'd run from the town to tell you about chickens?

ANNA. Well there's nothing else going on is there? You ran up here to tell me about that frog last week.

JANE. I didn't run about the frog.

ANNA. Yes you fucking did.

JANE. I hurried. *I hurried* to tell you about the frog and anyway when was the last time you saw a frog?

ANNA. This morning.

JANE. That's not true.

ANNA. Oh my god Jane you're not the only person that notices things!

MARIELLA. I wonder if he'll kill her.

ANNA *and* JANE *stop and look at her.* ANNA *vibrates with anger.*

ANNA. Mariella, shut up.

MARIELLA. Treason is serious Anna.

ANNA. Kings don't kill their wives! It's not – it just doesn't happen, alright?

MARIELLA. There's a lot of stuff that kings don't do that he ended up doing for her.

ANNA. Exactly. He's obsessed with her. And anyway, she's the Queen, what's she gotta do *treason* for?! Treason's for nutters, for losers!

JANE. Well apparently, Father said that last year people thought she tried to kill the King, at a dinner. They'd been arguing and then out of nowhere he started choking on his wine and people reckon she'd poisoned his / his what's it called

ANNA. Oh fuck off did she – / No she didn't

JANE. what's it called – his…

ANNA. *Cup* Jane! You're struggling for the word *Cup*! It's three letters!

MARIELLA. I wonder what she did when they arrested her, do you think she cried?

JANE. I'd cry.

ANNA. You cry at everything. She wouldn't have cried.

MARIELLA. It would take a very brave woman not to cry.

ANNA. She is a brave woman.

MARIELLA. How do you know?

ANNA. She's the Queen! Look at what she made him do for her!

MARIELLA. Boldness is not braveness.

ANNA. Her boldness is what made him fall in love with her! She'll be released! She *is* released! This is old news, tired news, it's done, it's boring.

MARIELLA. Perhaps it was just a punishment for not being with child.

ANNA. She's had one already.

MARIELLA. Not the right kind of one.

ANNA. It's not a crime to have a girl is it?

MARIELLA. Is if you're a queen.

JANE. She should have tried harder. My sister slept with garlic in her pillows every night and she's had only boys.

ANNA. Well they say she lost loads.

JANE. Father says women always say that.

MARIELLA. Which entrance did she take? In the Tower? Which gate did they take her through?

JANE. Well apparently it was y'know, the bad one.

MARIELLA. Knew it!

ANNA. Traitors' Gate?! They took her through Traitors' fucking Gate?

MARIELLA. Right well she must have done something bad then! Cos he wouldn't have put her in there for no reason would he? I mean she's the Queen! People love her, d'you remember when she was coronated? People were obsessed with her. Anna changed her hair.

ANNA. I did *not* change my hair.

MARIELLA. Yes you did! When she was made Queen you changed your hair!

ANNA. Mariella, I'm sorry if I like to experiment with style, some of us care about our appearance!

MARIELLA. I care about my appearance – hey maybe she killed someone!

JANE. Women don't kill people!

ANNA. I dunno I could probably kill Abigail Hayward.

MARIELLA *laughs*.

JANE. Well Father said that even before she was Queen, she used to take men to bed, scores of men and apparently *that's* what it is. She's been *loose*.

ANNA. Oh shut up Jane.

JANE. I'm *just* saying what other people are saying. I'm just saying what other people said.

ANNA. Yeah like a fucking child! She's not done anything with any men. Men fancy her, it's not a crime to be fancied is it? She's the Queen. Men always fancy a queen. She'll be released, I'm sure of it.

MARIELLA. Well you can't be *sure* of it, can you? It's not like we're there is it?

ANNA. We should be there, instead of *stuck* here where nothing happens.

JANE. Things happen here.

ANNA. No they don't Jane. We sit and talk about shit happening elsewhere, that's all that happens here.

MARIELLA. She saw a frog last week that's something.

ANNA. Y'know what, maybe I'll go. Yep, maybe I'll steal a horse and I'll ride all the way to London and I'll slip off its back in thin-soled shoes and I'll take hot buns from the market and fall in love with some tall handsome dangerous man and / he'll kiss me

JANE. Dangerous?

ANNA. Yes.

JANE. Why's he got to be dangerous?!

ANNA. Oh! Sorry shall he be a baker? Shall he be a *farmer*?

JANE. I just don't know why he's got to be dangerous, why can't he be nice?

ANNA. NICE?! Because Nice is boring! What good is nice?!

JANE stands, suddenly very flustered.

JANE. Alright fine, go on then.

ANNA. Go on then what?

JANE. Go and meet your dangerous criminal but don't come crying to me when it all goes wrong.

ANNA. Mariella! You heard her don't come crying to her when it all goes wrong!

MARIELLA. Oh Jane please let me come crying to you when it all goes wrong! Wait c'mon we're joking! Where are you going?!

JANE. I have to go, I have to get ready.

MARIELLA. Get ready for what?

JANE. Dinner.

ANNA. What 'Dinner'?

JANE. Just dinner. I like to get ready for dinner sometimes.

Beat. Something's off. MARIELLA *peers at* JANE, *studying.*

MARIELLA. Oh my god. She's washed her neck!

JANE. No! No I haven't!

ANNA. SHE'S WASHED HER NECK! WHAT'S HAPPENING?!

JANE. IT'S NOTHING. It's nothing!

MARIELLA. JANE! TELL US NOW WHAT'S GOING ON, WHY HAVE YOU WASHED YOUR NECK?!

JANE. Father says I'm to wed soon, that's all!!

MARIELLA. WHAT?! What do you MEAN that's all!! Oh my god! Oh my god Jane that's amazing! Who?!

JANE. The eldest Waitley boy, Richard? From Alresford?

MARIELLA. The farmer?! Oh Jane, well *done*.

JANE. I know! He's nice, well he seems nice, he was at the Mayfair dance. Apparently it's been in the works for a while, with his family.

MARIELLA. Good fucking work from your dad to be fair.

ANNA. Why didn't you say?

JANE. What?

ANNA. About the marriage. Why didn't you say when you got here?

JANE. Oh, I don't know... you know what it's like, nothing means anything until it means something.

MARIELLA. Well it's *great* news, isn't it Anna?

ANNA. Sure.

MARIELLA. And think of the *food*! Think of the food you'll do! Chicken!! Maybe a pie! Oh do a pie!

JANE. You don't approve.

ANNA. Of marriage?

JANE. Of the match.

MARIELLA. Of course she does.

ANNA. I didn't say anything.

JANE. I can tell by your face.

ANNA. What about my face.

JANE. You're doing your cruel face.

MARIELLA. She's just thinking about what she'll wear.

ANNA. I'm just surprised that's all.

JANE. Why? He's a good man. His family are respected. They own a lot of land.

ANNA. Exactly. He lives a fast life doesn't he? A man like that, goes to the London markets, travels around, I just thought maybe he'd need someone a bit more –

JANE. A bit more what?

ANNA. ... nothing.

ANNA shrugs and JANE blusters, the silence is more hurtful than any word.

JANE. and anyway, I don't want to wait any longer. Y'know, I want –

ANNA. what do you want? You want a baby in your belly is that it?

JANE. I want to live.

MARIELLA. Y'know, maybe the heat will break soon.

ANNA. You would do well to dream a bit Jane.

JANE. Dreaming is not living. It's not. It's just thinking. It's just *thinking*, about living.

ANNA laughs but it prickles at her skin, this truth from JANE.

ANNA. You think I just *think* about living do you? You think I don't *do* anything?

MARIELLA. That's not what she said.

ANNA. and what, tending to your husband, cleaning his shoes, making his dinner, that's living is it?

JANE. Just cos it's not a life you want don't mean it's not a life.

ANNA. No, I'm sure you're everything he wants in a wife.

This feels like a punch to JANE's chest, she won't cry in front of ANNA.

JANE. Well, I should go. I don't want to be late.

MARIELLA. We should all go, I mean it's very hot.

JANE. It's very hot.

ANNA. Y'know I think, I've gotten used to it.

Blackout.

Scene Three

Days later.

RICHARD *fucks* ANNA *up against a tree. They finish, he pulls his trousers up as she pulls her skirts down. She watches him but he looks at the sky. She picks up a flask and drinks deeply from it.*

RICHARD. It's *so* fucking close. God, has it ever been this hot before?

ANNA. Please don't talk to me about the fucking weather.

They both laugh. She drinks from the flask and then hands it to him.

Here.

RICHARD. Y'know that's *my* water.

ANNA. Yeah which is why I'm being very generous and offering you some.

He takes the flask, he drinks, she watches him.

RICHARD. Where's the bracelet?

She looks at him, smiling, playfully, makes a mock 'Hm?'

The bracelet I gave you, where is it?

ANNA. Oh! I didn't fancy wearing it today.

RICHARD. What are you, bored of gifts now?

ANNA. Well you can have *too much* of a good thing.

RICHARD. You're getting too many now is that it? You didn't tell me I was competing!!

ANNA. Oh you're *always* competing, didn't you know that?

RICHARD. I bought it so you could wear it.

ANNA. What you think I need jewellery to be beautiful?

RICHARD. I don't think you need anything to be beautiful. So I could *see* you wearing it in the market and know you were mine.

ANNA. Well, who's to say it'd be your one I'd be wearing?

He SWIPES for her but he misses and she cackles with laughter.

AH TOO SLOW!!!

RICHARD. You're a fucking tease, you know that?

He laughs and then turns and continues getting dressed. She swallows, leads up to it.

ANNA. You never said, about Jane.

A souring silence.

RICHARD. Didn't I?

She shakes her head. He sighs, uncomfortable. Scratches his head. Frowns.

Look, Anna, it's not in my control. I didn't even think we'd end up going through with it.

ANNA. But you are? Going through with it?

RICHARD. Yeah. We are, yeah.

ANNA. I mean I don't care.

RICHARD. This was always a casual / thing

ANNA. I know. I was just asking. I don't care.

Beat. She nods. He nods.

She's nervous though.

RICHARD. Is she?

ANNA. Yeah, she thinks you're too handsome for her or something.

RICHARD. I don't think that's true.

ANNA. Course not, she's stupid.

RICHARD. I think she's very pretty actually.

Beat. ANNA *wants to glass him.*

ANNA. Yeah… her hair's bad though.

Beat.

I mean I love her but it is.

He watches her and then snorts with laughter, it makes her want to kill him.

What?

RICHARD. Nothing.

ANNA. So, we should stop this now. Seeing as you'll be, y'know, doing *this* with her soon.

RICHARD. You should find someone, while there's time.

ANNA. You make it sound like the tide's coming in.

RICHARD. No, just, y'know.

She smirks at him.

ANNA. What you think you're the only one?

A flicker of irritation sparks in his mind, the way she's smirking, the way her eyes are blazing.

RICHARD. Am I not?

ANNA. Well I don't know if you heard but John Pollen's in love with me.

RICHARD. Is he?

ANNA. Not jealous are you?

Beat. He feels a flicker of annoyance and decides to ruin it.

RICHARD. He won't marry you, Anna, you know that right? He's had a contract signed for him since he was a boy.

She opens and closes her mouth, humiliated, red in the face.

ANNA. I'm not saying I want to *marry* him. I – he's a fucking baker, he wants me.

He laughs again.

What?

RICHARD. Nothing.

She watches him. She wants to punch him now, really.

ANNA. So do you fancy her then? Jane?

RICHARD. You know I don't.

ANNA. I don't know, maybe you do, maybe you've been thinking about her this whole time.

RICHARD. Anna, c'mon. I'm just trying to do right by the farm.

ANNA. She's worth a lot then.

RICHARD. Not really. But y'know, she's, she's a good girl, good stock, good family, I don't know what you want me to say.

ANNA stares at him, her eyes blazing.

I'll want you. I'll not stop *wanting* you, ever.

She stares at him, willing him to kiss her, he moves forward to do so and she relishes putting her hand on his chest to stop him.

ANNA. I thought you needed to go.

RICHARD. Anna.

ANNA. You *said* you needed to go.

She can feel his want for her pulsing through his chest, she can feel it in the palm of her hand, the power. She enjoys it.

And you'll be married soon remember? To Jane? So you should go.

RICHARD. Fine.

ANNA. So if you see me in the market you'll have to try and not go red.

He nods, smiles. He looks around for his jacket, dissolving the tension between them.

RICHARD. Yeah, well I'm not in the market this weekend anyway so.

ANNA. No? Where are you?

RICHARD. London. It's chaos up there, people are losing their fucking minds.

ANNA. Why?

RICHARD. The Queen, obviously. I mean it's fucking big Anna.

ANNA *stares at him, blank.*

ANNA. But is she not, is she not *out*? Now?

RICHARD. Why would she be out?

ANNA. Because, she's the Queen?

RICHARD. Yeah well not for much longer. I mean they've arrested like, twenty men or something.

ANNA. Why?

RICHARD. Why'd you think? Apparently *all* of them have been with her, have had her. They reckon she manipulated the King, forced him, blinded him into the marriage.

ANNA. Blinded him?! He changed the law so he could marry her! He rearranged the world so that she could be his wife. That's not blind, that's, that's like, loads of paperwork! For years!

He laughs.

RICHARD. Yeah well I'm not saying she didn't play the game well.

ANNA. So, what, what you think she's guilty?

RICHARD. I dunno. The way she's been, the way she's behaved, implies she's guilty.

ANNA. Well, y'know when I was fifteen, I thought I killed a dog.

RICHARD. You thought you killed a dog?

ANNA. I was running very fast and it started running with me – it wasn't chasing me – just by my feet and it was a tiny little thing and it got under my legs and I fell and kicked it down the ravine, you know by Alresford? It tumbled all the way down and I didn't stop – I saw it but I didn't stop.

RICHARD. You kept going.

ANNA. And I felt terrible for days and the pastry cook told me she could sense a shift in me and I laughed but really I thought 'that's cos I'm a dog murderer. I'm a dog murderer' and I told Abigail Hayward I was a dog murderer and then two days later I saw the dog and it was alive. Great. But by that point Abigail Hayward, that bitch, thought I was a dog murderer and told everyone I was and even now people reckon I have killed a dog.

RICHARD. Great. Is that…?

ANNA. That's it, yeah.

They both laugh.

RICHARD. It's a good thing you're beautiful.

ANNA. I'm just saying, sometimes just cos you *act* like you're something doesn't mean you are that thing.

RICHARD. Yeah well that's the *point*, she wasn't what she was *supposed* to be. Look, I have to go.

ANNA. Okay then, go.

He laughs at her, she doesn't move. He steps forward, she moves back, out of reach.

RICHARD. Fuck.

ANNA. Sorry. Forbidden fruit now, remember?

He shakes his head, completely enraptured. She laughs, she can tell how frustrated he is and she loves it, the power, all thought of Jane gone.

RICHARD. Fine. Bye then.

He turns to walk away and she relaxes, and then he steps back and catches her, kisses her, deeply, intensely, roughly, catching her off-guard, his grip tight on her arm.

Too slow.

He lets go of her, laughs and walks off, and she can still feel the pinch of his fingers on her arm.

Blackout.

Scene Four

MARIELLA *is stood running her hands over an engraving on the tree trunk.* ANNA *is shelling peas but is unable to focus, she throws them down, starts pacing.*

MARIELLA. When did we do this?

ANNA. Do what?

MARIELLA. This. The letters. The letters on here.

ANNA. I dunno do I.

MARIELLA. I don't remember doing it.

ANNA. Some years now. I dunno.

MARIELLA. Did we all do it?

ANNA. What? Yeah probably.

MARIELLA. Are you sure we *all* did it? It doesn't look like my handwriting.

ANNA. Well how often do you carve letters into trees Mariella?! Really?!

MARIELLA. Alright, I was just asking!

ANNA. and I'm just saying!

MARIELLA. Look why don't you just sit down for a bit.

ANNA. No I can't sit down. I can't do anything.

MARIELLA. Well pacing is something.

ANNA. Do you have to be this irritating every single day?

MARIELLA. This is who I am.

ANNA. Can't you change it? If I was your husband you would change it.

MARIELLA. Yes well you'd strike me. You'd be stronger than me and could make me change it.

ANNA. I *am* stronger than you.

MARIELLA. Not true.

ANNA. I'm a year older than you.

MARIELLA. So?

ANNA. That means I'm stronger.

MARIELLA. Are you fucking dull in the head?

ANNA. I'm older so I'm smarter and stronger. That's how it works. Look at children.

MARIELLA. What do you mean?! What do you mean look at children?!

ANNA. Erm, they're younger and weaker?

MARIELLA. That's cos they're children! If a babe of two years is stronger than you it would be witchcraft!

ANNA *rushes over and they tussle, both trying to drag the other to the ground.* MARIELLA *is stronger and she wins.*

ANNA. FINE! Fine! Fucking hell – fine!

MARIELLA. Look, I hate to say it but honestly / you have to

ANNA. If you hate to say it then don't fucking say it / then

MARIELLA. You are gonna have to settle your humour. You are wild, too wild. It's like being friends with a fucking horse.

ANNA. Oh fuck off Mariella.

MARIELLA. I'm *serious*, you need to calm down a bit, for your own good.

ANNA. For my own good?

MARIELLA. Lucy Jackson got beaten by Edwards for talking back the other day.

ANNA. So?

MARIELLA. They reckon the men are changing.

ANNA. Men don't change. Oh look here she comes! COME ON!!

JANE is approaching offstage. ANNA is very excited.

COME ON! COME ON! HURRY UP. RUN. JANE RUN.

MARIELLA. Don't make her run. JANE DON'T RUN.

JANE arrives, desperately out of breath, poor bloody Jane.

ANNA. Well?!

JANE. First, let me –

ANNA. Let you what let you what?! Light a fire? Knead some dough?! Just tell us!

JANE. All guilty.

Silence. The wind out of them.

ANNA. *All* of them?

JANE. Brereton, Norris, Weston and the other one – Mark Something, he was at her court, a musician, a lute player. But apparently Brereton, Norris and Weston say they're innocent, that they didn't do it.

MARIELLA. but not the lute player?

SCENE FOUR   37

JANE. No, he admits guilt. He admits, what's it called, *adultery*, with the Queen.

MARIELLA. Fucking hell.

ANNA. Well he would admit it wouldn't it? Boys say shit like that all the time, doesn't make it true.

JANE. He wasn't bragging, apparently he cried throughout his entire chat.

MARIELLA. It's not a *chat* Jane it's a trial. His poor mum.

JANE. Father says she'll be hung too probably. Although the King is said to be merciful.

ANNA. Why are you talking like that?

JANE. Like what?

ANNA. like a prick 'the King is meant to be merciful' what does that mean?

JANE. I'm just *saying* what people have said.

MARIELLA. So that's it then, that's treason. She's fucked.

ANNA. How is it *treason*?

MARIELLA. I told you! Because she – if she slept with some man, what's-his-name the lute player and she got pregnant then it wouldn't be the King's blood would it? She'd have put some other line on the throne.

JANE. Yep and I think the fact that the lute player admitted it, there must be *some* truth in it cos he would be tortured, right…?

MARIELLA. Don't use that word!

JANE. So he wouldn't have said it for no reason. Apparently London is *mad*, apparently the French fashion has dropped off a cliff since she fell out of favour, Father says he saw a woman burning her dress in the street.

MARIELLA. Well I never suited the French fashion, so that's a win for me really.

ANNA. I'm sorry but they think she wanted to kill the King and put a *musician* on the throne?

JANE. Perhaps.

ANNA. A *musician*?

JANE. Is it so strange?

ANNA. He's a musician, Jane. He's a lute player, that's not even one of the good ones.

JANE. Maybe she got carried away.

ANNA. WHAT WITH A FUCKING *LUTE* PLAYER?!

MARIELLA. Well he'd be good with his hands wouldn't he?

JANE. And it wouldn't be the first time she's done something like that!

ANNA. Oh my god not this again / I can't listen to it

MARIELLA. Jane's right, it won't look good. Especially on top of the Henry Percy thing.

ANNA. She was engaged to Henry Percy years ago, way before she even met the King, it doesn't count!

MARIELLA. It *always* counts.

ANNA. Not if nothing happened, women are engaged all the fucking time and nothing ever happens, it's the past.

MARIELLA. The past can be changed.

ANNA. Not if there were witnesses!

MARIELLA. Anna, he's the King. He owns everything, past and future. They will say that Henry Percy had his way with her. They will say that she wasn't a virgin when she met the King, that she was loose and then she continued to be.

ANNA. Are we forgetting that she *gave* Percy up?! Isn't that proof that she loved the King?! Cos I would not have given up someone I loved for anything, I would have told Henry to fuck off.

SCENE FOUR 39

JANE. What and risk displeasing the King of England?

ANNA. Yep, I'd have told him to take his gammy leg and his double chin and piss off.

MARIELLA. Well that's easy to say when you've got nothing to risk.

ANNA. Erm my beauty?

MARIELLA. Your beauty?! Fuck off! You wouldn't risk your beauty for anything.

ANNA. Yes I would!

MARIELLA. So, the King comes to town and tells you to marry him or he will scar your face and you would push him away and say 'no thanks I'm going to marry – John Pollen or Thomas Cotley or'

JANE. Or George Hatchworth

MARIELLA. 'Or George Hatchworth, or Mark Stanley thank you very much take all your jewels and your balls and your dances and slice my face open, I'm not giving them up.'

ANNA. Correct.

MARIELLA. You're SUCH A LIAR!

ANNA. Love isn't something to be discarded like a habit Mariella! It's a birthright, it's land, it's it's air, it's the sky! It's the storm!

MARIELLA. Who said that?

ANNA. Me.

MARIELLA. There is no way you just came up with that.

ANNA. I just came up with it right now! I'm very fucking poetic! If anyone ever lets me be!

Half a beat –

No one *understands* love around here that's the problem.

JANE. That's not true.

ANNA. Yes it *is* true Jane.

JANE. No it isn't. People understand love here, I've seen it.

ANNA. Where have you seen it?

JANE. In Mariella.

Beat – air shift – even ANNA *feels bad, and flicks her eyes at* MARIELLA.

ANNA. Well, yeah, *obviously* and look at how that ended.

MARIELLA. Can we not talk about it please?

JANE *kindly changes tack.*

JANE. Well, I would've been happy to have married the King, I'd have said yes immediately.

ANNA. Course *you* would Jane, you've wanted to marry him since you found out how often they have pigeon.

JANE. It's my favourite one! I don't understand how you don't like it.

ANNA. You wouldn't survive at court.

JANE. Why not?

ANNA. Do you know how much they drink? One cup of wine and you'd be on the floor.

MARIELLA. Anna you tripped over your own skirts summer last / if you forgot

ANNA. I WAS DRINKING ON AN EMPTY STOMACH. WHICH, MARIELLA, was your fault!

JANE. Well if the news about the pigeon is true then I wouldn't be drinking on an empty stomach would I?!

MARIELLA. I just don't think it makes any sense, a queen and a lute player.

ANNA. Unless she was forced. Maybe he forced her.

JANE. he's just a boy.

MARIELLA. Boys can be forceful. She's still only a woman.

JANE. Well Richard says she's not the type of woman that needs to be forced.

> ANNA *stares at* JANE, *she frowns, her heartbeat racing, it feels like the world has jolted.*

ANNA. What? What's that mean?

JANE. He just says, that the way she got the King wasn't good.

ANNA. It was clever.

JANE. Women don't need to be clever they need to be *good*.

ANNA. Since when?

JANE. Since always.

MARIELLA. Well maybe she didn't have a choice. It's not like she could've said no to the King, not really.

JANE. Of course she had a choice. She chased him for *years*. She designed all of it and look what she was like, she made him divorce Catherine, and I heard the other day that the day she found out Queen Catherine died, Anne Boleyn wore white and ate grapes standing up.

MARIELLA. That does sound like a lie Jane.

JANE. Father doesn't lie.

ANNA. All men lie. And if Anne Boleyn came into the village, every man in Essex would be knocking down her door. Trust me.

JANE. Not any more.

MARIELLA. So what happens next then? If the men have been found guilty? Now what?

JANE. They're all to be killed.

MARIELLA. When?

JANE. I don't know, Father left London two days ago.

ANNA. So maybe they're already dead then.

They are silent and think about this.

How can we live this way? As if everything has already been written, as if what might happen has already happened.

MARIELLA. And the Queen? What about her?

ANNA. Well he might let her out now.

JANE. No she's still in the Tower. She's to stand trial.

MARIELLA. God, she must be terrified.

ANNA. She must be furious.

JANE. She must be starving.

Blackout.

Scene Five

ANNA *and* RICHARD *have finished having sex, she's pulling down her skirts. She watches him as he gets ready, he won't look at her.*

ANNA. Anything?

RICHARD. I haven't been to London in days.

ANNA. Why not?

RICHARD. Reasons. Things.

ANNA. What things?

RICHARD. I dunno, just things, men things.

ANNA (*laughing*). 'Men things'! What are '*men* things'?!

RICHARD. Y'know what I mean, like, wedding.

ANNA. Your wedding?

SCENE FIVE   43

RICHARD. Anna, can you not?

Beat. ANNA *stares at him. Burning with sudden irritation.*

ANNA. You know it was *you* that asked me to come here.

RICHARD. Yeah well you still came didn't you?

Beat. ANNA *can't respond to this – he has a point. She tries again.*

ANNA. Y'know, people are saying she'll be released soon. The Queen.

RICHARD. No one's saying that.

ANNA. Yes they are. Now the men have been punished, they think she'll be released.

RICHARD. Well that's, that's, not how it works is it?

ANNA. How what works?

RICHARD. Justice.

ANNA *laughs at him and it makes him want to kill her.*

ANNA. Justice! Justice for what?!

RICHARD. For what she's done Anna! I mean, she's done some disgusting things, unwomanly things.

ANNA. Yeah well maybe I'd do some unwomanly things if I was stuck listening to the King all day. Maybe she was bored. Maybe she snapped. Men always think they're more interesting than they are, maybe his poetry was shit and she was tired of pretending like he was smarter than her.

She catches him staring at her.

What?

RICHARD. Nothing, just –

ANNA. Just what –

RICHARD. You should watch yourself Anna, all this, it's not good.

ANNA. Since when have you wanted me to be good?

He smirks, acknowledges the point. ANNA *won't stop.*

Anyway, you said she was beautiful once.

RICHARD. No, I never said that.

ANNA. Yes you did.

RICHARD. I would never *say* that.

ANNA. Yeah in the graveyard you said she looked like me.

Beat. It's tense. And then ANNA *snorts with laughter. It makes* RICHARD *want to punch her.*

Well, I should probably go. I have *many many* people who want to see me. Love letters to read. Stories to tell. Sunlight to stand in and so on.

He's staring at her.

What? Are you gonna tell me I'm beautiful in this light?

He doesn't say anything.

Oh! Where are my sweets? You promised sweets *weeks* ago. Are you worried if you give me them my teeth will rot and you won't want to kiss me any more?

RICHARD. Why were you running?

ANNA. What? When?

RICHARD. That story you told about killing the dog. When you were fifteen, you said you were running.

ANNA. I didn't kill the dog.

RICHARD. No, of course not.

ANNA. That was the *point* of the story.

RICHARD. Yeah

ANNA. I wouldn't kill a dog.

RICHARD. But what were you running from?

ANNA. Did I say I was running from something?

RICHARD. Yeah you said you were running from something.

ANNA. I think I was just running.

RICHARD. What for no reason?

ANNA. What were you doing, taking notes?

RICHARD walks over to a bush and plucks some berries from it, rolls them in his hand.

I can't remember.

RICHARD. Right.

ANNA. It was *years* ago.

RICHARD. Sure.

ANNA. What would I be running from?

RICHARD. I don't know do I?

Beat.

ANNA. Richard.

RICHARD. How many men have you been with?

ANNA stares at him. Shocked by the question. Then he starts laughing.

Do you not know the number?

ANNA. What are you doing?

RICHARD. It's just a question. It's just…

Beat.

I've heard a number.

A silence. She can feel something coming.

Well, I should go.

ANNA. I'm not doing this again, I mean it. This is the last time.

He nods, unconvinced.

RICHARD. You should probably stop calling her Queen by the way, they're not calling her that any more.

ANNA. What are they calling her?

RICHARD. 'The Great Whore.'

He smirks. ANNA *feels winded. He leaves.*

Blackout.

Scene Six

WILLIAM *stands facing the sky, facing away from us. He has a brace of dead hares slung over his shoulder, their blood crusted. His hands are touching the tree, his fingers on the carving of Mariella's name.*

And then JANE *blunders in and he jolts out of whatever memory he was in.*

WILLIAM. Oh / sorry

JANE. Oh! Sorry! I didn't realise / someone was

WILLIAM. No, not at all! I was just erm – I was just taking a moment under the… erm…

He looks at the tree, he's forgotten the word 'tree'. He's fucking forgotten the word 'tree'.

JANE. …tree?

WILLIAM. Tree! Sorry! Yes! The Tree! I was under the tree, it's very – it's very hot.

JANE. Yes, it's very hot. Too hot really.

WILLIAM. Yes, too hot, definitely.

JANE. Rabbits!

WILLIAM. Hares. They're hares. Not that it's – important – no, I erm, well it's silly really we have people to do it but I still like to go out and hunt them myself. Good to be out.

JANE. Yes.

WILLIAM. They mate for life!

JANE. Oh.

He's embarrassed her. He can see that he's embarrassed her. He feels bad.

WILLIAM. Yep. So! I, I hear congratulations are, are in order!

JANE. Yes, yes thank you!

WILLIAM. Your father must be very happy.

JANE. Yes very happy, very happy yes.

WILLIAM. He's a good man, Richard. I don't know him well, but his family are, are good people, good land.

JANE. Yes, a very good man. I'm very lucky – grateful.

WILLIAM. And it's alright to be nervous.

JANE. Is it?

WILLIAM. Of course. But it's, it's a wonderful thing to be married… in the end.

JANE *smiles at him. She wants to fill the silence.*

JANE. Yes how is Eleanor doing?

WILLIAM. Good! Tired but good. Nervous but but, very good. Eating a lot and sleeping a lot and y'know, shouting a lot. She's, taken to eating lots of, of bread in gravy and says her tongue tastes like iron.

JANE. Mariella says the taste of iron means it's a boy.

WILLIAM. Does she?

He nods. In his pocket, he fiddles with a token, a thing of the past, runs his hands over a memory of her, away from everyone. He makes every effort to say the next bit, so delicately, as if barely saying it.

Yes how, how is, Mariella?

JANE. Yes good. Busy. Agnes keeps her busy.

WILLIAM. Yes. Yes, I thought so. I've not seen her up at the house.

JANE. Your house?

WILLIAM. Yes, sorry my house, yes she's not – it was only Agnes, who visited, when Eleanor thought the baby was coming early – it wasn't – and well yes no Mariella, just, just Agnes, but...

But even at the market on Saturdays, I don't see her...

I can't seem to *ever* see her.

JANE *offers a kindness, unfurls it in the palm of her hand.*

JANE. Well I think there's a lot of women, expecting, in the area. So.

WILLIAM. No of course, of course. She's a midwife! They tend to be busy! But, but she's, she's well?

JANE. Very well.

WILLIAM. Good. Good. That's – that's good. Well I should go. But it was, it was *lovely* to see you and – and congratulations again.

JANE. Thank you.

WILLIAM. And good to, see that he's treating you so well already!

JANE *confused at him,* WILLIAM *nods at the bracelet.*

It's very beautiful. The bracelet. Is it turquoise? I think Eleanor would never shout at me again if I bought her something like that.

JANE. Oh, oh no, this isn't from Richard.

WILLIAM. Oh.

JANE. It's, it's Anna's, someone, someone gave it to her. Y'know what she's like, always getting gifts!

WILLIAM. Of course she is.

He stares at her for ever so slightly too long.

Well a bit of advice – most husbands don't like their wives wearing gifts from other men.

He's smiling but JANE *feels her stomach tighten.*

Just doesn't look –

JANE. No of course.

WILLIAM. Wouldn't want people to get the wrong idea.

JANE. Yeah, no, course not, sorry – it's, it's stupid. I don't know why I'm wearing it.

An awkward silence, he stares at her and smiles. JANE *smiles back but her heart is racing.*

WILLIAM. Well I should go but, congratulations again! And if you see her, tell Mariella, I'm, I'm glad she's well.

JANE. Of course, sir.

He smiles at her and walks off. JANE *turns and wrenches the bracelet off her wrist.*

Blackout.

Scene Seven

It's dusk, the night is bruising the sky. It feels like it might rain.
ANNA *is attacking the bush with a stick.*

MARIELLA *stands at the edges of the field by the tree, watching. Unsure of what to do. She's wearing her overcoat and bag. She wants to help but* ANNA *looks feral.*

MARIELLA. Anna?

ANNA. Go away!

MARIELLA. Anna, what's happened?

ANNA. Just fuck off Mariella! Fuck off!

MARIELLA. I can't fuck off! You're upset!

ANNA. I'm fine!

MARIELLA. Please don't do the whole 'I'm fine' thing it's – I mean / it's not true obviously

ANNA. No fuck please just / fuck off

MARIELLA. I'm not gonna fuck off alright?! I'm not, so stop, stop telling me to fuck off cos it's, it's really rude!

ANNA. Just leave me alone Mariella! I'm attacking this bush and I will be fine!

MARIELLA. Do you want a pear?!

Beat. ANNA *stops slightly and sniffs at her. She looks like a child, resting on her knees.*

ANNA. A pear?

MARIELLA. Yes, would you like one? I mean I've only got one but would you, do you want it?

ANNA. Where'd you get a pear from?

MARIELLA. The garden.

ANNA. Whose garden?

MARIELLA. I meant a field

ANNA. What field?

MARIELLA. Does it matter?

Beat.

Eleanor Updale's.

ANNA (*thrilled*). Mariella! WHAT?!

MARIELLA. I didn't take a good one! It was the worst one I could find!

ANNA. Still took it though!

MARIELLA. It's the worst one. I bet it's watery and mushy. She would've chucked it.

ANNA. You'll get in trouble for that.

MARIELLA. It's *one* pear.

ANNA. Women have died for less.

MARIELLA. and you've got away with more.

ANNA. I thought you weren't going to their house, thought you were getting out of that one?

MARIELLA. Yeah well turns out Agnes has got eyes in the back of her head so turns out I *am* going there now.

ANNA *holds out the palm of her hand.*

ANNA. Okay, give it then.

MARIELLA. You feel sad and I understand but you don't have to be fucking rude.

ANNA. Fine, *yes* please Mariella *please* give me the pear that you plucked from dear Eleanor Updale's garden. Thank you so much. I am desperately grateful and you are a wonderful good woman. My gosh.

MARIELLA *roots around in her basket for it. She hands the pear to* ANNA. ANNA *bites into it.* MARIELLA *watches her.* ANNA *offers the pear to her, she takes it and has a bite.*

It's so good.

MARIELLA. It's so good.

> ANNA *swallows. She offers some of the juice off her hand to* MARIELLA *who sucks it.*
>
> Feel better?
>
> ANNA *nods.*
>
> Good.

ANNA. So, what did Eleanor do then? To make you take the pear?

MARIELLA. Y'know all that crying has made your cheeks a beautiful pink.

ANNA. Really?!

MARIELLA. Yes.

ANNA. Mariella *really*? Or are you just saying that?

MARIELLA. Really.

ANNA. cos you did say last week that my teeth looked yellow.

MARIELLA. Well you were being a cunt that day.

> *Beat.*
>
> I wouldn't lie about your beauty Anna, I know it means too much.

ANNA. It does. It means everything, people say it doesn't but it does.

MARIELLA. Shame it's being wasted on me and not some handsome man.

ANNA. I could run into town?

MARIELLA. Or if you're very fast you could steal a horse and get to London –

ANNA. If I cry the whole way perhaps my cheeks will still be pink by the time I get to the river.

MARIELLA. and the men will flock

SCENE SEVEN 53

ANNA. and the women will scowl

MARIELLA. and you'll be wed within the day.

They laugh.

She kicked me in the face, Eleanor.

ANNA. WHAT?!

MARIELLA. Yeah I know. Mad.

ANNA. She kicked you in the face?

MARIELLA. In the face, yes.

ANNA. Actually like fully in the face?

MARIELLA. Yes.

ANNA. Shoes?

MARIELLA. No. Barefoot.

ANNA. Oh thank god.

MARIELLA. Anna!

ANNA. Oh don't be so frightened Mariella, I'm *thanking* him not blaming him.

MARIELLA. You know the minister had Jessica whipped for blasphemy on Sunday –

ANNA. Oh my god, which Jessica – actually don't care – so Eleanor kicked you in the face, then what happened?

MARIELLA. Well it was very quick cos she was thrashing around a bit, y'know, primal. I *think* it was an accident.

ANNA. Yeah but was it though?

MARIELLA. Agnes says so.

ANNA. Did she kick Agnes too?

MARIELLA. Yeah in the neck.

ANNA. In the neck!

MARIELLA. I know.

ANNA. Fuck me. So she's had the child then?

MARIELLA. NOPE. She's not even done that! I got summoned cos Agnes, despite being older than fucking water *still* doesn't know how to make a poultice for a sweat rash. So *obviously* I had to go along with her to make it and then apply it to Eleanor's perfect little thighs like an idiot –

ANNA. Mate you should've kicked her back.

MARIELLA. I can't kick a pregnant woman Anna.

ANNA. *Back*. You can kick a pregnant woman back.

MARIELLA. I am not going to kick a pregnant woman in the face.

ANNA. not in the face.

MARIELLA. What like the leg?

ANNA. The arm?

MARIELLA. The belly?

ANNA. Mariella!

Beat.

MARIELLA. It wasn't *meant*.

ANNA. but it was *said*.

MARIELLA. You know I meant no harm.

ANNA. You're getting as bad as me. Don't let the men hear you speak like that, apparently a sense of humour is out of favour, along with every other fucking thing.

MARIELLA *stares at* ANNA.

Was William there?

MARIELLA. Erm, yeah. He's the one that sent for Agnes, apparently Eleanor had been restless in her sleep and that's when he saw the sweat rash, thought it was something else.

ANNA. I see.

A loaded silence

MARIELLA. I was *with* Agnes, Anna.

ANNA. I know.

MARIELLA. And it's my job.

ANNA. I didn't say it wasn't.

MARIELLA. Agnes says it happens all the time, as women get near the birth, rashes, sickness. They get nervous and it spreads through their sleep into their bodies.

ANNA. Is it that bad? I know women that have had theirs easily, back up in an hour.

MARIELLA. Depends on the child. Depends on the woman.

ANNA *nods, tentative, gentle.*

ANNA. They share a bed then? William and Eleanor.

MARIELLA. Evidently so.

ANNA. Perhaps as the baby nears, he thought it would be better to be close to her, like any husband –

MARIELLA. Anna you don't need to do that. She's his *wife*. It's of little consequence if they share a bed or not.

ANNA. How can you bear it? I would *die* from the pain. He loves you.

MARIELLA. He *married* her! He was always going to marry her.

ANNA. But he doesn't –

MARIELLA. Oh do we always have to make it about men?! Is there nothing else to talk about? Is this all there is?!

ANNA. Of course not! We can talk about my beauty if you like?

MARIELLA. Or what made you attack the bush?

ANNA *sighs, relenting. It takes her a while, to say the next line.*

ANNA. Mariella, have I got ugly? You can tell me, I can take it.

MARIELLA. You can't take it.

ANNA. Have I? But have I?

MARIELLA. What's happened?

ANNA *shakes her head.*

ANNA. Do you think she'll still get out? The Queen?

MARIELLA. What?

ANNA. Do you think, do you think she'll still get out? D'you think he'll let her out?

MARIELLA. I, I don't know. Maybe.

ANNA. I just – none of it makes any sense. He waited seven years to marry her, carved her name across the country, doesn't that mean anything? Doesn't that count for anything?

MARIELLA. What's wrong?

MARIELLA *stares at* ANNA *as she shakes her head, as she tries to explain how she's feeling.*

ANNA. I just feel like, like I'm being boiled down? I feel like I'm being reduced over a very hot fire into something, small and and hard and I don't know *why*? I can't work out why? Like, I can't work out when it changed? Everything I do, seems, seems wrong and – it feels like the air is changing, is the air changing?

Silence.

MARIELLA. No.

ANNA. No?

MARIELLA. *No.* It's just a weird time. It'll pass. And anyway what does a king's marriage matter to us? Really? Nothing.

ANNA *nods. She isn't convinced but she nods.*

ANNA. Yeah. Yeah, you're right. I know you're right.

ANNA *flops back down.*

Urgh, fuck *me*, I just, I just *hate* people.

MARIELLA. Yeah, me too.

ANNA. Who do you hate the most?

MARIELLA. What one person?

ANNA. Yeah. Go on, who do you hate the most like who would you wish dead?

MARIELLA. Anna to speak this way is not, it's not good.

ANNA. Mariella! Tell me who you hate the most! Tell me it's Eleanor Updale!! If you don't tell me right now I will cry and scream and hurl my body on to the ground at your feet –

MARIELLA. Yes! Okay! Fine! It's Eleanor!

ANNA. and can I just confirm it's ELEANOR UPDALE?!

MARIELLA. Yes!

ANNA. Of 'Updale Hall'

MARIELLA. I can confirm I hate Eleanor Updale of Updale Hall!

ANNA. Who kicked you in the face?

MARIELLA. Who kicked me in the face.

ANNA. For apparently no reason?

MARIELLA. For apparently no reason.

ANNA. and took the love of your life?

Beat. Too far.

MARIELLA. He made me no promise Anna.

ANNA *stares at her, shrugs her shoulders.*

And you? Who do you hate? The most. In all of England.

ANNA. It's tough because I hate so many people. Can I say all men?

MARIELLA. Only if you mean it, which you don't.

ANNA. My father?

MARIELLA. Your father doesn't count. Everyone hates their father.

ANNA. Jane doesn't. She's obsessed with hers; it's fucking irritating.

MARIELLA. You should be nicer to her. It's a big thing what she's going through, marriage.

ANNA. The way she's acting lately, sleeves down, head bowed / all pious

MARIELLA. She's a good girl, you can't despise her for that.

ANNA. I don't *despise her*! I feel sorry for her! All that effort to be good and she'll be married to a man who'll chase after other women!

MARIELLA. You don't know that.

ANNA. Men don't want girls like Jane, Mariella, come on.

MARIELLA. Her getting married doesn't mean you won't.

ANNA. What? I'm not worried about getting fucking married – I could get fucking married Mariella, I'm the one who's being proposed to, it's me saying no to them. I don't care.

MARIELLA *nods, thinks*.

MARIELLA. Sometimes I have this dream – not even a dream just a thought – imagining what it'd be like if they didn't exist. Men. Would it be better? Maybe it'd be better. I'd see less pain. I'd see less blood. And I think, I sort of think I'd hear the birds more? Yes I think I'd hear the birds more and look at the ground less, if there weren't as many men around. Wouldn't it be great? No engagements. No contracts. No *marriages*. No sex. Just us, just women.

ANNA. God I'd be so fucking bored.

MARIELLA. No you wouldn't.

ANNA. Yes, I would. Men are – men are doors to somewhere else Mariella. To be able to get a man to stare at you or want you, or choose you that's, power. And it's the best kind, cos it's inside of you, if you've got it, you can't lose it, it's not like having money then not having money. If a man wants to fuck you, he'll give you anything you want, do anything you want, they pretend like it's not true but it is true, I know it is and it's fucking delicious.

MARIELLA stares at her and smiles, takes her time, gently – she might even reach out, touch her hand.

MARIELLA. You know, you really should stop talking like that.

Blackout.

Scene Eight

A few days later. Sunshine. Sheets are drying on the tree. ANNA is leading JANE in a dance, MARIELLA is stood watching.

JANE. And then what do I do?!

MARIELLA. You go to your left.

JANE. Which left?

ANNA. *Your* fucking left! Obviously!

MARIELLA. Anna, don't be a bitch!

ANNA. I'm not being a bitch she can't work out her left or right!

JANE. I'm trying to! But it's a lot to remember actually

ANNA. No! No! You're doing it wrong! Put your arms down. Look I do it like this and then when you come to the front of the line look – eyes are down eyes are down eyes are down and then *bam* they're up.

JANE. Then what happens?

ANNA. They fall in love with me.

MARIELLA. Brilliant, of course they do.

ANNA. It's all in the eyes and it's all in the arms

MARIELLA. Why is it in the arms?!

ANNA. Men love arms, they remind them of their – *y'know.*

MARIELLA. WHERE have you heard that?

ANNA. Everyone knows that! So Jane remember, just keep the rhythm – Mariella, give us a clap.

MARIELLA. What d'you mean give us a clap?!

ANNA. Just give us a clap!

MARIELLA starts clapping a rhythm.

Clap better!

MARIELLA. WHAT DO YOU MEAN?!

ANNA. JUST CLAP FUCKING *BETTER* MARIELLA!

ANNA spins JANE around laughing as MARIELLA claps on a rhythm.

Come on keep going!

ANNA leads them all around in a circle of dancing, skipping. ANNA leads the charge, she's making noises too as they all start clapping the same rhythm until eventually they stop and collapse on the floor laughing.

JANE. Oh, OH GOD do you think he'll pull out of the wedding if I can't dance?

ANNA. It is a possibility yes.

JANE. Oh I just want it to be over. Let it be over!

MARIELLA. No you don't want it to be over!! You're just nervous!! But once it's here, you'll have a great time!

JANE. What if something *happens*?

MARIELLA. What do you think is going to happen?

JANE. What if you know, what if I *need* to go?

MARIELLA. Go to the toilet before.

JANE. What if I can't go?!

MARIELLA. Thought you could always go?

JANE. Not when I'm nervous!

ANNA. You could just get drunk, that'll stop you being nervous.

MARIELLA. She shouldn't get drunk at her own wedding. Jane you'll be fine.

ANNA. I mean you'll be *terrible* but you'll be fine

JANE. Do I have to do *it*?

ANNA. Of course you have to! It's your wedding night! We can practise if you like?

JANE. Erm no thank you.

ANNA. Get you a simple man from the market

JANE. You shouldn't joke about that.

ANNA. Could get you Edward Harris, although you'd have to like it rough

MARIELLA. and dirty

ANNA. and smelly

MARIELLA. and you'd have to face his wife.

JANE. I don't want practice!

MARIELLA. We're joking! We're obviously not going to drag Edward Harris here!

ANNA. I mean would he come?

MARIELLA. Oh I think he always *comes* Anna.

JANE. You shouldn't joke about that!

MARIELLA. Oh Jane it's not like anyone can hear us!

JANE. I just don't want him to think I'm like *that*.

ANNA. Like what? Oh! Oh like the Great Whore?!

MARIELLA (*laughing*). Oh Jane! Come on! You can't be serious / she

ANNA. You know she believes it? What they're saying about the Queen?

JANE. No I didn't say I *believed* it!

MARIELLA. What?! No you don't! Jane! Come on!

JANE. I'm just saying he's been arrested! Why would he have been arrested if he wasn't guilty of it?! All the others were!

ANNA. He's her brother! She wouldn't sleep with her own brother, she's not a fucking animal!

JANE. Well Richard says some girls will open their legs for anyone.

MARIELLA. Brother's still a bit far Jane.

JANE. He said he wouldn't be surprised if she'd slept with a hundred men, the way she is, and that once this is over, the King should get himself a new wife, a simple god-fearing woman.

ANNA. What, plain like you, you mean?

MARIELLA. Anna!

Beat. MARIELLA *stands and checks the drying sheets.*

ANNA. What – ? Oh come on I'm just joking. She knows! I'm *just* joking!

JANE. It's fine.

SCENE EIGHT   63

ANNA. Oh don't – fucking – do that.

JANE. What?

ANNA. The fucking victim thing like, don't 'it's fine. It's fine'.

JANE. I'm not doing anything.

ANNA. Yes you *are*. I can feel it.

MARIELLA. OKAY! These are ready!

ANNA flopping on grass.

ANNA. NO! No they're not!! They're not!

MARIELLA. Well they are! So off you pop before you get into trouble again OH! BUT! I have some gossip for you if you want it! Heard it in the butcher's!

ANNA. Oh my god yes, yes please!

JANE. No! No I don't wanna know, I don't wanna know!

MARIELLA. You don't know what it is yet!

JANE. I'm not taking part in, in gossip any more!

MARIELLA. Jane we just spoke about the Queen shagging her brother!

ANNA. She didn't shag her brother.

JANE. That's not gossip that's news. And I'm soon to be a wife and Father says men want women who pray more than they talk. So I can't be gossiping about my neighbours any more, I'm turning over my leaves.

Beat.

MARIELLA. What?

JANE. My leaves. I'm turning over my leaves.

ANNA. Your leaves?

JANE. Yes I'm turning over my new leaves. You know, starting over.

MARIELLA. Jane, you – you only get *one* leaf.

JANE. What?

ANNA. It's turning over *a* new leaf.

MARIELLA. It's not like – you don't get a *series* of leaves.

JANE. What?

MARIELLA. Yeah the expression is 'I'm turning over a new leaf'.

Beat.

JANE. But… I already turned over my leaf last year when I stopped biting my nails.

ANNA *and* MARIELLA *stare at her.* JANE *loses it.*

What so *that's it*?! What I get one leaf and that's it?! I get to turn it over what, once and and that's it?!

ANNA. and you barely even bit your nails.

JANE. but that's not fair!

MARIELLA. Life isn't fair.

JANE. But I'm trying to be good! I'm trying to be better! I deserve more leaves!

ANNA. We all deserve *more* leaves Jane!

JANE. Well I might as well know the gossip now. Go on.

MARIELLA. Apparently, Abigail Hayward broke a plate so her master made her eat off the floor. Mad right? Like a dog.

ANNA *gasps in delight.*

JANE. That's awful.

ANNA. It's not that awful! Abigail's a bitch and she's always going around pretending she's this pious little thing and she told everyone I murdered a dog!

MARIELLA. But *did* you murder the dog?

SCENE EIGHT 65

JANE. I like Abigail. She's nice, she's good.

ANNA. You don't know her.

JANE. Yes I do. We talk.

ANNA. What d'you mean you talk? Since when do you talk to people?

JANE. I have other friends Anna.

MARIELLA. and you speak to Abigail do you?

JANE. Yes.

ANNA. Where?

JANE. In the market.

ANNA. When?

JANE. When I'm with Father.

ANNA. Classic.

MARIELLA. What's classic?

ANNA. Jane and her fucking dad.

JANE. What's wrong?

ANNA. You spend too much time together. It's weird.

JANE. When I have a house of my own I'll need to go to the market myself. It's practice.

ANNA. It's stupid.

MARIELLA. Practice isn't stupid.

ANNA. being good at going to the *market* is stupid.

JANE. being good at being *good* is smart. It's what they want.

ANNA. How do you know what men want Jane?

JANE. Because *I'm* the one that's going to be wed to one.

A hard beat. Lines being drawn.

MARIELLA. Jane.

ANNA. Does your dad ever mention your dowry to you?

JANE. What?

ANNA. On these little walks to the market where you practise being good does he mention your dowry?

JANE. Why do you care?

ANNA. I'm just asking. Must be very exciting, must be very *persuasive* for Richard.

JANE. What's that supposed to mean?

ANNA. Just that it must be very persuasive for him, if you come with money.

JANE. Well it's not my fault you don't Anna.

Beat.

ANNA. I don't – I wasn't *asking* about the dowry cos I care about money, I've never cared about money – I was just – y'know what, fuck this, I have to go.

She begins to pull down the sheets from the tree.

MARIELLA. Anna –

ANNA. Nope! These are ready remember! And some of us have a million different things to do! We can't all just sit here, talking about – about *nothing*.

ANNA *bundles the sheets into her arms*.

JANE. Wait. Here.

JANE *holds out* ANNA*'s bracelet*.

I should've given it back weeks ago, I'm sorry.

ANNA. No, it's fine I gave it to you, you can keep it.

JANE. Oh, no I couldn't do that, it's yours.

ANNA. I don't care.

JANE. Anna, would you just take the bracelet? Please, I don't want it.

Hard beat.

It's just, it's not *appropriate* for me to have it.

MARIELLA. Jane, it's just a bracelet.

JANE. I just don't want people to think –

ANNA. Think what?

JANE. I shouldn't be wearing things from men that aren't Richard, it doesn't look good.

ANNA. Well you didn't get it from a *man* you got it from me.

JANE. It's immodest Anna.

ANNA stares at her, fury bubbling away, laughs but doesn't have any words to say, she thinks of some but there's a lump coming up her throat, so she snatches the bracelet off of her.

ANNA. Fine. If you're gonna be a fucking –

MARIELLA. Anna, she's just trying to –

ANNA. I know what she's trying to *be*, Mariella. I'm going.

ANNA storms off. MARIELLA *turns to look at* JANE *intensely and* JANE *holds up her hands.*

JANE. What?! I didn't do anything! I can't walk around with it on!

MARIELLA. You know that stuff means a lot to her.

JANE. Well maybe my father means a lot to me! She shouldn't be allowed to just – just say whatever she thinks about people and just get away with it! And it's not weird me and Father, it's, it's nice.

Beat.

We've actually got a hand thing we're gonna do at the wedding.

MARIELLA. A hand thing?

JANE. Yeah, me and Father, like a hand dance? Richard's big on hands.

MARIELLA. Is he?

JANE. Yep.

MARIELLA. Well that sounds brilliant.

JANE. I will be happy I think.

MARIELLA. You will be happy.

JANE. and you will be too, one day.

MARIELLA. I'm lucky I'll always be needed.

JANE. and wanted.

MARIELLA smiles at her, she doesn't want to have this chat any more. She gets up.

MARIELLA. Right, well I better go, every girl in Essex seems to be fucking pregnant at the moment.

She goes to leave and JANE fiddles with something on the tip of her tongue.

JANE. Can I ask you something?

MARIELLA. Course.

JANE. Are you sure?

MARIELLA. Oh my god Jane / please

JANE. Am I sexy?

As in, as in, I know I'm not amazing, I know I'm not Anna

MARIELLA. Don't say that.

JANE. She's right, about me being plain isn't she? I mean I know what she's saying, under it all, she's saying he won't fancy me

MARIELLA. No she isn't. She's just, that's just Anna. Ignore her.

JANE. But am I? Am I, sexy enough?

MARIELLA. Course you fucking are. Oh Jane, listen he's going to find you so sexy and, so, so beautiful and funny, it's going to be brilliant. It's going to be lovely.

JANE. Will it hurt?

MARIELLA. Maybe.

JANE. Will I feel different after?

MARIELLA. Probably.

JANE. A proper woman?

MARIELLA. Something like that.

JANE. Okay.

MARIELLA. Okay?

JANE. Okay.

MARIELLA goes to leave and it bursts from JANE.

They're saying stuff about Anna.

MARIELLA turns around to face her.

MARIELLA. Who is?

JANE. People.

MARIELLA. In the town?

JANE. Yes.

MARIELLA. Who?

JANE. Women.

MARIELLA. Well women have never liked her.

JANE. and the men.

Hard beat.

MARIELLA. What are they saying?

JANE. Just, stuff.

MARIELLA. What stuff Jane?

JANE. I don't wanna say.

MARIELLA. Don't open the door and then not fucking walk through it.

JANE. Just that she's fast, that she's been with some men.

MARIELLA. So?

JANE. Men she shouldn't have been with.

MARIELLA. Names?

JANE. Thomas Cotley, obviously. George Hatchworth. John Pollen.

MARIELLA. William?

Beat.

JANE. Of course not. She'd never do that to you.

MARIELLA *shakes her head, looks around, embarrassed at the panic.*

Her master, maybe.

MARIELLA. Aldward? *Aldward?* That's what they've said?

JANE. That bracelet is expensive. William said it's, it's proper turquoise, that's not the kind of thing she'd get off, off a baker or something. That's a wealthy man's gift or – or a married man.

MARIELLA. But Aldward?

JANE. She said about sleeping in his bed remember! Ages ago! She said about sleeping in his bed! She never gets in trouble with him! And you've, you've heard how she talks about, about men.

MARIELLA. She wouldn't do that.

JANE. Really?

MARIELLA. Not unless he forced her.

JANE. I don't think you need to force a girl like Anna.

MARIELLA *stares at* JANE.

MARIELLA. No one will marry her.

JANE. Richard said no one would marry her anyway. He said who would buy a horse that's not in need of breaking in.

MARIELLA. Jane.

JANE. Look, they burnt two women, two villages over, in Colchester.

A shocked silence.

MARIELLA. Well, Colchester is not here and it was probably for witchcraft.

JANE. It was for adultery.

Beat.

Apparently, their husbands did it.

MARIELLA *feels the bottom of her stomach drop out.*

MARIELLA. But that's not the law.

JANE. The law can be changed, remember? Sometimes I think I can feel something coming at night. Sometimes I catch women looking at her in the road, men staring at her in the market. Sometimes I look at her and all of her beauty has gone.

MARIELLA *stares at* JANE, *thinks about her own life.*

MARIELLA. You're nervous, you just need to sleep. There have *always* been women like Anna.

JANE. Will you speak with her?

MARIELLA. and say what?

JANE. I don't know, warn her about what's being said.

MARIELLA. We don't even know if it's true

JANE. Lots of people are saying it

MARIELLA. well lots of people said you had four nipples and that wasn't true was it? And you nearly burnt for that!

JANE. are people still saying that?

MARIELLA. Jane, please! Just go home! I'll speak with her!

Blackout.

Scene Nine

The sun is going down, the air close. Somewhere else, thunder rumbles, it looks like it might rain.

ANNA *waits, she's calm, tired.*

She hears him coming and turns to look as RICHARD *strides in, furious.*

ANNA. Look, I know it's late / but I

RICHARD. Don't *ever* fucking do that again!

ANNA. What are you talking / about?

RICHARD. Coming up to me in the market, talking to me like that. Looking at me like that in front of people, in front of her whole family, her / dad

ANNA. I didn't realise they were / there

RICHARD. Oh you always know when people are there Anna don't fucking lie. I marry her tomorrow what the fuck is wrong with you, are you thick? Are you, are you dull in the head?!

ANNA. I wanted to see you / I had to talk to you

RICHARD. Yeah well you don't get to do that. D'you hear me? You don't get to decide when I see you. I'm not your, your little fucking dog that you get to just, just *summon* and / I'll come fucking running

ANNA (*laughing*). I didn't *summon* / you at all

RICHARD. DO *NOT* LAUGH AT ME!

She's shocked at the outburst, she stares at him. A silence.

I won't have you fucking laugh at me, not any more. I mean it. I won't.

He readjusts himself.

Now, what is it? What do you want?

ANNA. Don't marry her.

Beat –

RICHARD. What?

ANNA. I don't want you to marry her.

RICHARD. You don't *want* me to marry her?

ANNA. I'm not asking you to marry me, I'm just asking you not to marry her. Pick someone else.

RICHARD. What is this?

ANNA. I, I just / I don't

RICHARD. You in *love* with me or something?

ANNA. No, no of course / not

RICHARD. Want me to marry you is that it?

ANNA. ... No / ...

RICHARD. Pick you?

ANNA. That's not what I meant.

RICHARD. That's what you said.

ANNA. I... / just...

RICHARD. Why would you say it if it's not what you meant?

ANNA. Richard, I / just

RICHARD. Or are you just doing it cos you think you can?

ANNA. What?

RICHARD. Trying to get in my head, get under my skin, trying to, to fuck with me? To try and prove you've got some kind of, of power over me? Bringing me here, trying to ruin my life, her life, for no reason?

ANNA *explodes* –

ANNA. Oh my god you don't even fucking fancy her!

RICHARD. What?

ANNA. You don't! I know you don't! You're just, just doing as you're fucking told, you're like a little boy it's, it's pathetic!

RICHARD. I would watch how you speak to me.

ANNA. Well it's, it's true isn't it? You won't admit it but you, you don't, you don't want her, you want me, you've always wanted me / you

RICHARD. Want you? You think I want you? Anna, look at the state of you.

Beat.

ANNA. Alright well I'll tell her then. I'll tell her. I'll tell her, I'll tell everyone, I'll tell her family, your family. I'll stop it, tell them what you are, that you begged me to meet you here, you asked me to come –

RICHARD. Are you *threatening* me?

ANNA. And they'll call off the wedding, and you'll lose your precious dowry, and your, your virgin wife and your fucking perfect fucking – and you'll lose me, cos I won't come here any more, I'll find someone else, I'll marry someone else and / you'll have to watch

RICHARD. Marry? Who you gonna marry Anna? What, John Pollen? Thomas Cotley? They won't marry you, you know that.

ANNA. I've, I've had a lot of offers…

RICHARD. Ah, c'mon, that's not true. You've had a lot of men, won't deny that but not, not offers of marriage. They've all had you in a field why would they want you in a bed?

Silence.

Ah, what you think we don't talk? Oh men talk Anna. And they talk about *you*. About what it's like to be with you. About what it *feels* like. I don't, I could but I don't. But I will, I will if you ruin this for me.

ANNA. You, you were the one that wanted me. You were the one that kept, kept asking me to come.

RICHARD. Never said no though, did you? I mean, do you *ever* say no? And anyway what, you think it'll make a difference? Who asked who? You think she'll believe that? Believe you?

ANNA *is rooted to the spot.*

No, you're not the type of girl women believe Anna, you know what type of girl you are. You've *shown* me, what type of girl you are.

Beat.

And now you're standing there, when I've had the decency not to talk about you, and you're threatening me? Where do you think you are? What do you think this is?

Somewhere else, thunder rumbles. ANNA *knows, that there is no other option.*

This is *England* woman.

Blackout.

Scene Ten

Wedding music, the sound of laughter, jubilation.

Eventually MARIELLA *walks out, she's got a cup in her hand maybe, flowers in her hair. She comes and stands at the tree.*

She breathes deeply, taking a moment, and then WILLIAM *comes out after her.*

WILLIAM. Ah, I wondered who took all the wine.

She turns to look at him.

MARIELLA. Yep.

WILLIAM. Very well executed.

MARIELLA. You want some?

She nods. He nods. She hands him the bottle, he swigs, he passes it back.

Hello.

WILLIAM. Hello.

Awkward.

What a day for it.

MARIELLA. I know.

WILLIAM. Not too hot.

MARIELLA. No, not too hot.

He moves in closer.

WILLIAM. Are you having a good time?

MARIELLA. I am. I am. Are you?

WILLIAM. I am. Good food. I liked the pigeon.

MARIELLA. Did you?

WILLIAM. Oh, didn't you?

MARIELLA. No I did, I did. I just – didn't know if you liked it.

SCENE TEN 77

WILLIAM. You were sat with Anna?

MARIELLA. Yes. They shoved us in a corner. Away from the wine.

WILLIAM. She looked a bit –

MARIELLA. Drunk? Yeah. And you were sat with John Po–

WILLIAM. John Pollen. Yes. Good man.

MARIELLA. Very good man.

WILLIAM. Ate fourteen chicken legs though.

MARIELLA. What?

WILLIAM. I know. On the seventh I thought 'slow down John' but he just kept going.

MARIELLA. Fourteen?

WILLIAM. I know.

MARIELLA. But not *actually* fourteen.

WILLIAM. Mariella, I counted. I gave him mine on number twelve because I wanted to see how far he'd go. If the dancing hadn't started he'd be on number forty-five by now, no question. He went and started talking to Abigail Hayward and he was still holding the bone in his hand, like a knife.

MARIELLA. Like a knife!

They both laugh.

WILLIAM. And what did you, what did you think of Jane and her father's hand thing?

MARIELLA. Don't ask me what I think of the hand thing.

WILLIAM. I thought it was good.

MARIELLA. You didn't think it was good.

WILLIAM. I did! She's got excellent knuckles! I'd never noticed before!

MARIELLA. You know they practised? Every day?

WILLIAM. Of course they did. Did you see Richard's face?

MARIELLA. I know.

WILLIAM. I thought he looked impressed.

MARIELLA. Or terrified, god at least she's happy.

WILLIAM. As she should be, it's her wedding day. Most important day in a woman's life.

A bruised silence.

So, how *are* you?

Slowly.

You can't avoid me forever Mariella.

MARIELLA. I *think* we were avoiding each other.

Slowly.

I'm good. Really good.

Beat.

I'm *Better.* You?

WILLIAM. Better. Yes. Better.

He nods, she nods. A long silence.

I wanted to say, I'm so, sorry you had to come to the house the other week, with Agnes. I just, I was so worried about Eleanor's / rash and

MARIELLA. Please don't do that.

WILLIAM. Mariella –

MARIELLA. Will, *please* don't do that.

MARIELLA *stares at him and then slowly unravels a difficult truth.*

It could never have been me and that's fine

but it doesn't mean I have to forgive her and I know she didn't do anything and it's just the way the world is but it doesn't mean, that I have to stand here and listen to her name in your mouth.

He nods.

WILLIAM. Okay.

She nods, turns away for a moment to recollect herself.

We should get back.

MARIELLA. Yes.

WILLIAM. I should go back.

But they don't move for a moment. She stands and puts her hands on her hips. He stands and he puts – very gently – his hand on the nape of her neck. She likes the feel of the pressure, he knows she likes the feel of the pressure.

They stand there, his hand on her and look at the life they might have had.

ANNA *arrives and has the grace to not intrude.* WILLIAM *sees her and takes his hand away.*

I'm going to go back.

MARIELLA *nods and walks to turn her face as* WILLIAM *nods at* ANNA *and leaves.*

ANNA. I came to find you.

MARIELLA wipes her face and turns back to face her.

MARIELLA. Well you have, so well done.

ANNA. What's happened?

MARIELLA. Nothing, nothing new. What's happening in there?

ANNA *goes to sit down.*

ANNA. Nothing. Jane and Richard have finished dancing, and now some masked players have arrived.

MARIELLA. Masked players? He paid for *masked* players?!

ANNA. I know.

MARIELLA. That's a bit much, I mean he's only a farmer, who does he think he is?

ANNA *laughs*. MARIELLA *laughs*.

ANNA. Oh I *hate* all of it, don't you?

MARIELLA. I know.

ANNA. The whole day. The whole day just so fucking *loud*.

MARIELLA. and bright! So bright and happy!

ANNA. And *so* boring. No one wants to have any fun, no one wants to *do* anything. I tried to ask about the Queen.

MARIELLA. Oh yeah when does her trial start?

ANNA. Exactly. Dunno. Could be today, could be yesterday, who knows. No one will talk about it. As if she doesn't exist, as if *it* doesn't exist. 'Not appropriate' apparently.

MARIELLA. Did you see how many chicken legs John Pollen ate?

ANNA. No.

MARIELLA. Fourteen.

ANNA. Fuck off.

MARIELLA. Fourteen. One after the other.

ANNA *makes a noise of disgust,* MARIELLA *enjoys it.*

Apparently he's all over Abigail Hayward now. So you did well to avoid that.

ANNA. What?

MARIELLA. I thought you said he was in love with you?

ANNA. I *think* I said he used to give me free loaves.

MARIELLA *watches her.*

MARIELLA. Saw you talking to George Hatchworth.

ANNA. Yep. He kept telling me he'd never noticed how big my eyes were, 'like plates'

MARIELLA. Like plates! God they're *so* stupid!

ANNA. You should've seen his face, thought he was a fucking poet. Although he *is* handsome.

MARIELLA. Come on, we should get back.

ANNA. No! Don't make me go back in there! Please let's stay a bit longer!

MARIELLA. What if we miss her leaving?

ANNA. Oh my god Mariella, she's not going off to France, she's going to the fucking *marriage* bed.

MARIELLA. She's nervous.

ANNA. She's *always* nervous.

MARIELLA. He put his hand on her knee did you see? When they brought all the food in? To calm her down. He's nice isn't he? Sweet.

ANNA. Is he?

    MARIELLA *watches* ANNA *as she drinks*.

MARIELLA. Anna, are you alright?

ANNA. What's happened?

MARIELLA. Nothing.

ANNA. Do I not look alright?

MARIELLA. No you just seem –

ANNA. Seem what?

MARIELLA. I dunno.

ANNA. Just say it Mariella, what?

    Beat.

MARIELLA. I guess people are talking. People are talking about *you*.

ANNA. Well people are always talking about me.

MARIELLA. I guess it's a bit different. People are saying you've been with some men.

ANNA. yeah well obviously.

MARIELLA. No I mean…

ANNA. It's quite hard to *avoid* men Mariella. They're fucking everywhere.

MARIELLA. Anna, you can tell me.

ANNA's heartbeat races – does MARIELLA *know?*

ANNA. Tell you what?

MARIELLA. You can tell me, it's fine.

ANNA. Tell you *what*?

MARIELLA. If you're in trouble. If you're, doing things you shouldn't be doing. You can tell me.

ANNA. 'Doing things I shouldn't be doing'? What's that mean? *Doing things I shouldn't be doing* what's that even fucking mean?

MARIELLA. People are saying that you're going around with married men, that's what I mean. People are saying that you're letting married men fuck you and give you gifts, *that's* what I fucking mean Anna.

Beat.

ANNA. Well, that's not, that's not true. That's a lie and – and – you've got a fucking nerve, I walk in to you and William having the world's longest fucking silence and you've got / the audacity

MARIELLA. Don't fucking do that. We're very different.

ANNA. I haven't done anything alright?! And anyway, who's, who's saying that?

Silence. ANNA *can read it.*

Jane.

SCENE TEN

MARIELLA. She's just worried about you.

ANNA. Jane? Fucking JANE?! The girl who can't even remember the word 'cup'? She's an idiot!!

MARIELLA. Who's the bracelet from?

ANNA. What?

MARIELLA. The bracelet, who gave it to you?

ANNA. Oh my god, it's *just* a bracelet!

MARIELLA. No it's not just a bracelet and you know it's not. Jane said it was expensive, that it would've cost a lot, a wealthy man's gift so, so who gave it to you?

ANNA is backed into a corner, she doesn't know what to say.

Was it Aldward?

ANNA. Aldward? Of course not!

MARIELLA. Anna.

ANNA. Oh my god! Look it's just a fucking bracelet it doesn't mean anything! It's, it's cheap as shit, it's – it's nothing, here!

She pulls the bracelet out of her pocket and lobs it.

There! Happy? It means nothing! Was just given to me by some, some boy I didn't even know his name!

MARIELLA. You didn't know his name?

ANNA. Oh my god!

MARIELLA. Was he *married*?

ANNA. Mariella! Since when has any of this ever fucking mattered!

MARIELLA. Since they burnt two women in Colchester! Since they burnt two women for sleeping with married men! Their husbands dragged them out of their beds and out into the middle of the square and set them on fire and everyone watched, they *watched*, Anna.

Silence as ANNA *computes this, chews over her words, slowly.*

ANNA. Well, Colchester is not *here*... and I don't have a husband... and I'm not other women, am I?

Beat –

So that's not gonna happen to me.

Beat.

And I would tell you, if I was doing that.

MARIELLA. You would tell me.

ANNA. I would tell you, but I'm not.

MARIELLA. Good.

Beat – MARIELLA *is still angry but it comes out anyway.*

Because I love you.

ANNA. I love you too.

MARIELLA. And I don't want anything to happen to you.

ANNA. It won't.

They hug, maybe.

MARIELLA. Urgh, right. Come on then, we should go back in before she disappears. Do *not* let me have any more wine.

ANNA. But Mariella, how will you join in the hand dancing if you're not four bottles deep?

They laugh, they're about to go when a sudden noise catches on the wind. They turn and spot John.

What's that?

MARIELLA. Who's – ?

ANNA. Oh fuck off is that John Pollen. Oh my god it is! It is!

MARIELLA. Probably looking for more chickens.

Laughter.

SCENE TEN

ANNA. Is that Abigail Hayward?

MARIELLA. Oh my – No!

ANNA. It is! It fucking is! Oh my god, oh my god look at them go –

John grabs Abigail and begins to kiss her.

MARIELLA. Fucking hell – are they?!

ANNA. Wow her mum is gonna fucking kill her…

But then they stop laughing.

Because it's clear, that Abigail is not enjoying the sex with John. It's clear that Abigail is trying to resist. It's clear that Abigail is trying to get away. It's clear that John has her pinned up against the fence.

It's clear that John has got Abigail by the hair.

(*Whispers.*) Oh my god.

It's clear that Abigail is trying to scream but John has his hand over her mouth.

MARIELLA. Is he –

ANNA. Oh my god.

It's clear that Abigail is now on the ground and John is on top of her.

We have to do something – OI GET OFF OF HER!

His leg between her legs. His hand on her wrists. His other hand on her skirt, pulling it up.

OI!

ANNA *moves but* MARIELLA *stops her*

MARIELLA. ANNA DON'T! We need to leave!

ANNA. We can't just let him do that!

MARIELLA. Anna it's too late / we can't

ANNA. Mariella he's gonna fucking kill her!

MARIELLA. It's already happened! He's already done it! Come on, we have to *go*! Now!

> ANNA *looks back at Abigail and John one last time and then –*
>
> *Blackout.*

Scene Eleven

Lights up. Days later.

ANNA *is stood staring at the place where John Pollen raped Abigail Hayward. She's got some flowers in her hand. She's staring at it for a long time. Eventually* MARIELLA *comes in holding basket full of placenta- and blood-covered linens.*

MARIELLA. Anna.

> ANNA *turns to look at her.*

How long have you been out here?

ANNA. Oh, not long.

> *Silence. She doesn't have to explain because* MARIELLA *understands.*

MARIELLA. D'you hear that Abigail and John Pollen are engaged.

> *Beat.*

ANNA. What? After what he did to her?

MARIELLA. Apparently.

> ANNA *nods, swells up with the thought of it.*

ANNA. Y'know, I've been thinking, Mariella, I was thinking, I might leave? As in, go. I might go, somewhere else. Soon, when I can. Y'know, find somewhere new. I thought maybe

London, I've got some money, not loads obviously but, some.
I thought in a month or two, I could go, you hear about that
don't you? Girls who, leave and they get a room somewhere.

MARIELLA. That sounds like a good idea.

ANNA. I thought you could come with me. They'd need
midwives, loads of pregnant women in London, you could
train me. You know I'm a fast learner, only need showing
once. And we could go by horse, we could take hot buns
from the market

MARIELLA. and meet a handsome dangerous man?

ANNA. Yeah. Yeah, maybe. Or maybe just, maybe just a *nice*
man? Maybe just, a good man?

Maybe marry one? Then you wouldn't have to work, just,
just look after him.

MARIELLA. What make his dinner, wash his socks?

ANNA. Yeah, just be a wife, a good wife. Be a bit more like
Jane. That's, that's what they want, in the end isn't it?

MARIELLA*'s smile fades.*

MARIELLA. Yeah. Yeah, er, Agnes said she saw Jane in the
market this morning.

ANNA. Oh yeah?

MARIELLA. Yeah.

ANNA. I bet all that practice has come in handy now.

MARIELLA *smiles, weakly and then says the next bit so
delicately.*

MARIELLA. She reckons she had a black eye.

Beat – ANNA *looks at* MARIELLA.

I mean, Agnes said she only saw her briefly, might've been
a trick of the light.

ANNA. Right.

MARIELLA. Doesn't mean it's Richard.

ANNA. Doesn't it?

MARIELLA stares at her.

What will she do?

MARIELLA. I don't know. I guess the trick is to figure out what it was that made him hit you in the first place and then just not do that again.

ANNA laughs, nods.

ANNA. Has it always been like this?

MARIELLA. I don't know.

ANNA. Will it always be like this?

MARIELLA. I don't know.

They stare at the spot where John raped Abigail.

When will you go?

ANNA looks at MARIELLA – she was lost in a thought.

To London, when will you go?

ANNA. Oh, I don't know. Soon. Maybe now. Maybe today. You ready?

MARIELLA stares at her and smiles at her sadly, nods.

MARIELLA. Oh yeah. Absolutely.

MARIELLA and ANNA smile at each other.

Right well, I should get on with washing these, I was only cutting through.

ANNA. Disgusting.

MARIELLA goes to leave and then remembers to give one final warning.

MARIELLA. Maybe don't stay out in the dark, on your own? Just, in case people see. Get the wrong idea.

ANNA. I won't.

MARIELLA *leaves*.

Blackout.

Scene Twelve

Night.

The field is empty. ANNA *arrives, holding a lantern, she waits but no one is here. Eventually,* RICHARD *arrives holding a lantern.*

RICHARD. Anna.

ANNA. Fuck!

RICHARD. Sorry, sorry.

He laughs. She doesn't.

ANNA. I thought you were in London.

He puts the lantern down.

RICHARD. I was. I got back today.

ANNA. Well you can't just *summon* me. I'm busy, I've got stuff to do.

RICHARD. What have you found someone else already?

ANNA *shakes her head and goes to walk off.*

Wait wait wait! Anna / wait

ANNA. No / fuck off

RICHARD. Look, I got you something. I bought you something, please, please, please.

He holds out a package. Eventually she takes it.

Open it. Open it, open it.

She opens it, it's a packet of dusted sweets. She stares at them.

You wanted sweets right? Well these are the best ones I could find. Eat one.

She doesn't move, she just stares at them.

Go on, eat one.

She stares at him. She doesn't move.

Anna, eat the sweets.

ANNA. No.

RICHARD. Anna eat the fucking sweets.

ANNA. I don't want them. They look disgusting.

He can feel his temperature rising, his breath coming in deeper.

RICHARD. You're angry, okay. I understand.

ANNA. I thought you didn't want this any more.

RICHARD. Anna.

ANNA. I thought you wanted a wife.

She turns to leave and he rushes around to stop her.

RICHARD. Come on. You know that I miss you. I've thought about you. Every minute of every fucking day, I've thought about you. Please, I'm, I'm going out of my mind. Please Anna – you – come on, you're *killing* me. I've not stopped thinking about you, about your body, about your breath, your, *taste*. Anna, you should've seen me, you have to realise, I can't sleep, I've been, I've been hard under the dinner table, just thinking about your mouth –

ANNA. Where does she think you are?

RICHARD. She doesn't.

ANNA. You come back from London and you don't go home? That's pretty odd.

RICHARD. She doesn't say anything.

ANNA. Doesn't mean she doesn't think it.

RICHARD. Believe me, all she does is eat and pray and fucking, tremble. It does my head in.

ANNA. Stop hitting her.

Beat.

RICHARD. What?

She sits up and faces him.

ANNA. Jane. Stop hitting her. There's no need.

RICHARD. Where's this come from?

ANNA. I'm just saying.

RICHARD. Did she *say* that I hit her?

ANNA. She's been seen in the market with a black eye.

RICHARD. What you saw it?

ANNA. I heard it.

RICHARD. You heard it?

ANNA. I heard it.

RICHARD. But you didn't *see* it?

ANNA. I –

RICHARD. So you *heard* about a black eye, a black eye you never saw and you guessed *I'm* how she got it? I wouldn't do that Anna, if I were you.

She stares at him, she can see him.

ANNA. I'm not scared of you.

RICHARD. What?

ANNA. I said I'm *not* scared of you.

RICHARD. I, I don't want you to be scared of me.

ANNA. No I think you do. I think you like it. I think you enjoy it. But I'm not. And I just want you to know that I can see you, I can see who you are, I can see *what* you are.

He stares at her, he's not unnerved.

RICHARD. 'See me.' What d'you mean you can see me?

Silence. He smirks.

Come on Anna. You didn't come here, to tell me you're not scared of me, you didn't come here to tell me that I'm not what you want, or that I'm married, you came because you like what you do to me, you like the feeling of it, you like being what I want, you like the power I give you.

He's close to her, now, too close.

Just be honest with yourself.

He kisses her and she pulls away but only half, he keeps kissing her and it's intense and deep and eventually, it moves so that she goes with it, it's reluctant but it's happening. It's moving towards sex, it's moving, it's moving and –

And then MARIELLA *walks in and everything comes crashing down.*

ANNA. Mariella!

ANNA *pushes* RICHARD *off her as* MARIELLA *stands there in shock. No one moves, no one breathes.*

And then RICHARD *remembers that he owns the air and turns to face* MARIELLA.

RICHARD. She threw herself at me. If she does it again I'll tell Jane.

And he walks out.

MARIELLA *is breathing deep, fizzing with energy as she pieces it all together, as she tries to work out what's happened...*

MARIELLA. What have you done?

SCENE TWELVE

MARIELLA *can't believe it. She shakes her head.*

…no… no, no what have you done? What have you fucking done?

ANNA. I… Mariella

MARIELLA. Oh my god. Oh my god, the bracelet, it was him.

ANNA. It's not what you think, I, I can explain!

MARIELLA. You're out here with a lantern, he had his hand up your fucking dress, what's there to fucking explain?

ANNA. No I just meant it, it started before, before they were engaged

MARIELLA. And what about after, hm? What about *after*? What about two fucking minutes ago, what about two fucking minutes ago Anna? What about when I told you that she'd been seen in the market with a black eye? Your best friend, what about then?

ANNA. No, see I, I tried to call it off but –

MARIELLA. They're killing women for this shit now don't you fucking get that?! Can't you fucking see that?

ANNA. No, no cos that's, that's different, that's, it's, I'm not gonna be one of those women / I

MARIELLA. Yes you are! Yes you are! Look at yourself Anna, look at yourself! You *are* that woman.

Beat.

You are *already* one of those fucking women.

MARIELLA *shakes her head at* ANNA *in disgust and storms away.*

Blackout.

Scene Thirteen

Time passes. ANNA *tries to make herself smaller, better, a good woman. She tucks her hair away.* ANNA *wrings her hands and waits.* ANNA *is desperate for* MARIELLA *to come back.*

Lights down.

Scene Fourteen

ANNA *is still waiting, exhausted and tense, stressed. Finally* MARIELLA *walks in and stops – she just wants to cut through.*

ANNA. Mariella wait, please wait / please

MARIELLA. I don't want to talk to you.

ANNA. Mariella, just a few minutes please.

MARIELLA. I've been up since four, I want to go home.

ANNA. Mariella I just want to know if you've told her. Please, just tell me, have you told her?

Beat – MARIELLA *relents.*

MARIELLA. Of course I haven't told her, I haven't *seen* her.

ANNA. Are you going to?

MARIELLA. I don't know.

ANNA. Don't – Mariella, please, please just don't –

MARIELLA. She's got a right to know

ANNA. She doesn't have to know. Honestly, please, I've stopped, I promise.

MARIELLA. It's like you don't understand what you've done, what you're doing. He's her fucking husband Anna

ANNA. I know, I, I tried to call it off but –

MARIELLA. But what? He wanted you too much is that it?! He couldn't bear the thought of having to go back to her?

ANNA *doesn't say anything and* MARIELLA *laughs with the disbelief.*

Of course he did. How could Richard want Jane when Anna is alive? How could anyone?

ANNA. I knew you wouldn't understand

MARIELLA. Are you joking?! How do I not understand?

ANNA. Because *men*, men don't want you, the way they want me, Mariella! They just don't! I'm not bragging, it's been that way since I was a girl but –

MARIELLA. I can't hear this –

ANNA. No Mariella, please I know what you think –

MARIELLA. No, you know what I think Anna? D'you know what I really think? I think you don't even fucking know me. You don't. You're standing there and you've got the audacity to say that I don't understand? I don't understand?! After everything you saw me go through with William?

ANNA. No it's not the same – it wasn't about love –

MARIELLA. OH WELL FUCKING LUCKY YOU. LUCKY YOU ANNA, IT WASN'T ABOUT LOVE. But me? I've been walking around with a fucking limb missing, bleeding out all over the village and wiping it up before anybody sees it. Keeping my fucking eyes on the ground, trying to not see William in the sky or the sun or the hedgerow and you? You do this and it's not even for love? You just do this cos what? Cos you want to? Cos you can? Cos you think you're the only one? You think you're the only one whose body wants touching, wants fucking? I've loved him since I was eight and for the last two years I've existed on smiles in the market. You don't think I didn't want to be out here, out anywhere, with William?

ANNA. Then why didn't you?!

MARIELLA. Because it's not how the fucking world works! Because he married her! And what am I gonna do sabotage his life, sabotage mine? Because this way, at least I get to stand under the same bit of sky as him, breathe the same fucking air, because this way nothing gets ruined.

MARIELLA *stares at* ANNA, *seeing her for the first time. Takes her time.*

But you wanna know what I really think?

I think I'm jealous. I think I'm jealous that you can do that and it not even be for love. And I think I hate you for it. And I think I'm scared for you. And I think you're a marvel and a fucking abomination.

ANNA. It's not my fault you lost, Mariella.

MARIELLA. And you think *this* is winning do you? You think *this* is fucking winning?

JANE enters.

JANE. Have you heard?

They stare at her.

She's dead.

MARIELLA. Who?

JANE. Anne Boleyn.

A terrible silence.

ANNA. What?

JANE. I know.

MARIELLA. When?

JANE. Three days ago. Beheaded. At the Tower.

ANNA. Three *days* ago?

MARIELLA. Are you sure?

JANE. Of course I'm sure.

ANNA. What do you mean, three *days* ago? But – but when did the, she's meant to go on trial

JANE. She must've done.

ANNA. But *when*?

JANE. I don't know.

ANNA. So, she's just, she's just dead? So it's just, done? He's just done it?

A long silence.

MARIELLA. Is that even, is it even, legal?

JANE. It must be.

Beat.

Someone said she wore red.

ANNA. So? What does it fucking matter?

MARIELLA. What will happen to the baby?

JANE. What baby?

MARIELLA. *Her* baby. Elizabeth?

Heavy silence.

Do you think he'll… kill –

ANNA. No. No he wouldn't kill his daughter.

JANE. We didn't think he'd kill his fucking wife.

ANNA *and* MARIELLA *both look at* JANE, *she backtracks.*

Not that I'm saying, not that – I'm saying *he* did it.

ANNA. What?

JANE. Well *he* didn't do it, did he? It's not murder if, if she had a trial, it's justice, kings don't kill their wives for no reason.

A silence: is this true? Is this really, true?

He's married again apparently.

ANNA. What? Who?

MARIELLA. When?

JANE. A Seymour... Jane.

A sudden noise makes them all look.

MARIELLA. What's that?

JANE. They've kept the pubs open. The men are celebrating.

They all stare at each other, as somewhere else, men celebrate a whore who has been killed, toast to a virgin in a crown.

Blackout.

Scene Fifteen

Dawn.

JANE *stands by the tree, her hands using it for support, she's hyperventilating, deep breaths coming in and out, her whole face shaking.*

On the ground are the makings of a tincture, a pestle and mortar, herbs, a small pouch of dried leaves.

JANE *manages to calm her breathing down and she straightens just as* ANNA *walks in.*

JANE. Oh.

ANNA. Oh.

Beat.

Sorry... I...

JANE. No, I was just, I couldn't sleep. So I was just...

ANNA. Right.

JANE. Eleanor Updale's gone into labour

ANNA. Has she? Fucking hell, finally.

JANE. I know.

ANNA. Another Updale, I hope it doesn't inherit her chin.

JANE laughs but she doesn't find it funny. ANNA *looks at the tincture stuff.*

What are you...?

JANE. Oh, erm Mariella taught me it. Just a tincture, for, for making it *stick*.

ANNA. A child?

JANE. Yeah just to get some help, just to, give God a hand you know.

ANNA. So you're not sleeping?

JANE. No. I guess, I just... well I keep, I keep thinking about the Queen actually – not the Queen, Anne Boleyn.

JANE begins to speak but it's difficult, it's like the shedding of a skin.

I just keep, thinking about, about what *she* must've been thinking. About whether she knew, did she know, that her husband would do that to her? And if she *did* when did she know he was going to do that to her? Was it the day she married him? Did she look him in the eye and see it and ignore it? Was it the last day? Did she think he'd change his mind? Did she think *she* could change his mind? Do they ever change their mind, once they've decided to do something like that?

JANE stares at ANNA, *as if looking for an answer.*

ANNA. I don't know.

ANNA stares at JANE *and can't hold it back.*

Jane, please, your fucking eye / I can't pretend

JANE. I don't wanna talk / about it

ANNA. We have to / talk about it

JANE. It's not your business Anna.

ANNA. Not my business? Not my – *you* are my business Jane. You will *always* be my fucking business. He can't do that, to you. He doesn't get to do that to you, okay?

JANE. I'm his wife.

ANNA. It doesn't matter if you're his fucking wife he doesn't get to do it.

JANE stares at her and nods, it feels good to talk about it.

JANE. I think he hates me.

JANE tries to gather himself up.

ANNA. Hit him back. You should hit him back.

JANE. I think I hate him too, you know? I know I shouldn't say that, but, but I really think I hate him too.

ANNA. Good, cos he's a cunt.

JANE laughs at ANNA's boldness.

JANE. Shouldn't say that.

ANNA. Why not? Why shouldn't we fucking say it? He is. He's a cunt Jane. Say it!

JANE. He's a cunt.

ANNA. Yeah.

JANE. He's a real cunt.

JANE laughs again, watery and tear-filled but it's still a laugh and it relaxes and ANNA thinks about telling her, ANNA thinks that maybe she could tell JANE now and it would all be fine, it would all be alright.

But then MARIELLA arrives.

And everything in the world, changes.

Because MARIELLA *is shaking. Because* MARIELLA *is covered in blood. Her hands. Her skirt. Some on her face.* MARIELLA's *face is a twist of pain and confusion, sweat and dirt. She's still holding a cloth in her hand. They stare at her in shock.*

ANNA (*whispers*). Mariella.

JANE. Oh my god.

   MARIELLA *looks at both of them, trembling, terrified.*

MARIELLA. I will hang.

They move towards her, like she's an unexploded bomb.

ANNA (*whispers*). No, no you won't, you're okay / isn't she Jane, you're okay

JANE (*whispers*).Yeah, no you're / okay

ANNA. Just, just come here, come, over here.

JANE. What happened?

MARIELLA. She just slipped, she just *slipped* through my, my fingers I couldn't – I couldn't stop it, I *tried* to stop it but she just kept, kept *bleeding* and *bleeding* / and I

ANNA. Eleanor? Mariella? Are you talking about Eleanor?

   MARIELLA *nods, in shock, her body is still in shock, her hands still shaking.*

MARIELLA. She was just there and then she fucking wasn't / there

ANNA. Okay, it's, it's okay. It's – the baby, is the baby...?

JANE. Is the baby alive?

MARIELLA. Yes, it's, it's a boy I think

JANE. Well that's good, that's, a boy!

MARIELLA. I just had to get, the way she just, the way we all, the way I just watched her die.

ANNA. Okay

MARIELLA. I should've done something.

ANNA. No no no / don't do that

MARIELLA. I've killed her. I killed her. They're gonna, they're gonna come / for me

JANE. Mariella, no they won't

MARIELLA. It's Eleanor fucking Updale, her family own half the land around here! And she's dead, she's dead because of me.

ANNA. Not because of you! How because of you? Women die in childbirth all the time, all the time! This isn't, this isn't special and there's a *baby*! You saved the baby! It's a wonder you managed that!

JANE. And why wasn't Agnes with you?!

MARIELLA. Wivenhoe, one of the Mitchell girls went into labour I don't know

JANE. Well if Agnes had *been* there, like she was meant to be / then it would've

MARIELLA. But she wasn't there! She wasn't there! And I should have been able to do it alone!

ANNA. It's an accident

JANE. It's God's choice / who stays

ANNA. Jane, not now

JANE. It's *God's* choice, who stays and who goes.

ANNA. Mariella, nothing will happen, okay, it's an accident, a horrible accident but nothing / will happen

WILLIAM. What the fuck are you doing?

WILLIAM *has arrived.*

WILLIAM *too, is covered in blood, Eleanor's blood, his wife's blood. He's stood, his face impassive, any hint of charm gone, his eyes boring in to* MARIELLA*'s, shock reverberating off of his body.*

MARIELLA. William I…

WILLIAM. You have to come back.

MARIELLA. No.

WILLIAM. Now. You have to come back with me now.

ANNA. Sir you shouldn't be here.

WILLIAM. She has to fix what she's done.

MARIELLA. It cannot be fixed.

WILLIAM. You need to find a way.

MARIELLA. Please, please your mother is there, there are *other* women that can help you

WILLIAM. No it has to be you.

MARIELLA. Why?

WILLIAM. Because it was by your hand.

MARIELLA. She was already bleeding when I arrived!

WILLIAM. So you knew what was happening?!

MARIELLA. No that's not what / I mean

WILLIAM. You knew but you thought you would do *nothing*?

MARIELLA. Of course not / I would

WILLIAM. You knew but you let her die?

MARIELLA. No, no I would never

WILLIAM. You said you couldn't forgive her.

MARIELLA. What?

WILLIAM. You, stood there, at her wedding and said you couldn't forgive Eleanor, for marrying me, that you couldn't hear her name any more.

MARIELLA *realises where this is going, she shakes her head, she whispers the word 'no' but it doesn't come out.*

couldn't hear her name in my mouth, that's what you said, that you didn't *have* to hear her name in my mouth

MARIELLA. William

WILLIAM. And *now* she's dead.

MARIELLA. That's not what I *meant*

WILLIAM. That's what you *said*. That's what you *said* though Mariella, did you *will* this to happen?

MARIELLA. Of course not!

WILLIAM. Did you think that you might replace my wife?

ANNA. Sir / please

WILLIAM. Did you *think* you could end her life so you could take / her place

MARIELLA. William listen to yourself –

WILLIAM. / in *my* bed, at *my* table?!

MARIELLA. I –

WILLIAM. I should never have touched you! This, this is punishment! God is *punishing* me for / lying with you –

MARIELLA. You don't / mean that

WILLIAM. Women like *you*, you do no good! You bring shame and destruction and now look what you've done, you've murdered my wife!

ANNA. Watch your fucking mouth.

MARIELLA. Anna

WILLIAM. My mouth? You, the great fucking whore of the village tell me to watch MY MOUTH after what she's done –

ANNA. It was an accident!

MARIELLA. William, don't listen to her!

MARIELLA *goes to stop him lightly and he slaps her with such force it sends her to the floor*, JANE *immediately looks away, shaking, she can't watch.*

SCENE FIFTEEN   105

WILLIAM. DON'T TOUCH ME!

ANNA. NO!

Things happen very fucking fast, as WILLIAM *turns to hit* MARIELLA *again, he goes to grab her by the hair,* ANNA *throws herself on him, clawing at his back,* JANE *still facing away.*

GET OFF HER!

ANNA *pulls at* WILLIAM*'s arms and he turns to face her instead, and grabs* ANNA *by the neck, pushes her up against the tree. He's got his hand around* ANNA*'s throat.*

Please, I can't –

MARIELLA *staggers back to her feet.* ANNA *is thrashing, scratching at his hands on her throat.*

MARIELLA. Let go of her William please. WILLIAM! LET GO OF HER!

MARIELLA *is on her feet now. She's trying to get* WILLIAM*'s hands off of* ANNA*'s neck.* JANE *is frozen to the spot. Shocked at what she's seeing, appalled by the violence but unable to help.*

WILLIAM. You fucking –

ANNA *can't breathe.*

MARIELLA. William! Let go of her please!

ANNA *can't breathe.* ANNA *is scratching at his face and* MARIELLA *is pulling at his back, it's not working.*

JANE HELP / ME /

JANE. SIR / PLEASE

MARIELLA. JANE!

JANE *rushes to help and they manage to drag him off* ANNA, *who then leaps on him, too.*

WILLIAM. *GET OFF ME!*

And he turns and somehow as he turns ANNA *gets a grip, and as he goes for* MARIELLA *they all fall, a tangle together, arms flailing.*

JANE *falls away but the other two keep going, he's on the ground now.*

JANE. Stop. *Please!*

It is ugly as they thrash around but MARIELLA *and* ANNA *are winning. Their hands on his face and they keep hitting.* MARIELLA *stops but* ANNA, ANNA *keeps going and somehow at some point she's picked up* JANE*'s mortar, and she's cracking him over the head, she's punching him, over and over and over.*

MARIELLA *has stopped, watching in horror as* ANNA *keeps going and going and going and suddenly* WILLIAM *isn't moving any more, there's blood. There's blood all over him.*

ANNA.

MARIELLA. ANNA.

JANE. STOP.

And then suddenly ANNA *stops, as if she was in a daze. She stumbles back and they all fall into stillness.*

A terrible, heavy silence.

MARIELLA *is bereft, shocked, unravelling.* JANE *is shaking.* ANNA *stood, as if out of her body, panting.*

ANNA. Move.

WILLIAM *does not move.* ANNA *drops the mortar.*

William. *Move.*

WILLIAM *does not move.*

Tell him. Tell him to get up. Get the fuck up!

MARIELLA *drops down close to his body.*

MARIELLA. William! William? William, can you hear me?

ANNA. Mariella, get him up! Get him up *now*!!!

JANE. What have we done?

ANNA. Is he breathing? Check if he's breathing – he's –

MARIELLA. William!?

JANE. Oh my god –

MARIELLA. He's breathing, he's, Jane, go and get someone – Jane! Go! Now!

ANNA. No don't!

MARIELLA. What?

ANNA. She can't!

MARIELLA. What? What do you mean she can't? Anna he's barely breathing!

ANNA. Think! *Think* about what will happen, a man walks out into a field, to confront the woman who killed his wife and instead he ends up half dead. With the three of us here. Who do you think, who do you think *survives* in this situation? Who do you think *lives*?

MARIELLA *realises and she begins to shake her head*.

MARIELLA. No, no no / no no

ANNA. A dead man is less dangerous than a vengeful one.

MARIELLA. But this! This, this isn't just a man, this is, is William! It's WILLIAM.

ANNA. It doesn't make a difference.

MARIELLA. But he, he loves me and he's, he's a good man / he is

ANNA. What he loves you enough not to kill you? Not to blame you?

MARIELLA. He was upset and, and scared and you're wrong, I know you're wrong

ANNA. If I'm wrong then I'm wrong but if I'm right then we hang, Mariella. All of us.

Beat.

We need to leave. Now.

MARIELLA. If we leave, then he'll die! He'll fucking die! If I leave then I would've killed him!

JANE. She's right Mariella.

MARIELLA *looks to* JANE, *shocked.*

But, but we could warn someone. When we get to Alresford, we could tell someone where he is, I could tell someone where he is, so he'd be found, he'd be saved, he'd be fine.

ANNA. Yes. Let's do that. We can do that.

MARIELLA. You, you think we should leave?

JANE. Anna's right, he won't forgive you, they don't forgive, ever and what is left here for us, really? For any of us? And people will be looking for him already, her father, his uncle, they'll be looking for him and if they catch us, if they catch you...

MARIELLA *looks back at* WILLIAM, *trying desperately to process what's going to happen.*

ANNA. We could be in Kent by the morning, or London, I have money – we could get a cart, we could – maybe we could get a ship. Anywhere. Somewhere.

MARIELLA. And we'd tell someone where he is?

ANNA. They'll find him. I promise. Wouldn't they Jane?

JANE. Of course they would.

MARIELLA *thinks about it.*

MARIELLA. Okay.

JANE. Okay! Okay. Good. We're going. You both need to change.

ANNA. Why?

JANE. Look at the state of you! We'll get caught on the road, what good is running if we're caught two villages over, turn your dresses inside out.

JANE begins to undress MARIELLA as she still stares, shocked, choking back emotion. ANNA is undressing as quickly as she can. MARIELLA can't take her eyes off WILLIAM.

MARIELLA. I should have left when he married her. I should have got out of the way. I should've got out of his fucking eyeline, I shouldn't have stayed, if I had left then maybe...

JANE. Don't do that! Look at me, look at me you can't *do that* okay? Not now. We just have to leave.

ANNA is undressing as quickly as she can.

Anna, Anna you said you had money. Where is it – how much – ?

But JANE *stops speaking. She stops speaking because she is staring at* ANNA*'s body.* ANNA *has taken her dress off and is staring, breath deep, at both of them.*

ANNA*'s belly is swollen.*

Oh, Anna.

ANNA begins to turn her skirt inside out, she just wants to hurry this moment on.

ANNA. Can we not do this now?

JANE. Anna, whose is it?

ANNA. Please, Jane can we just leave?

JANE. We can't leave you've got a baby in your belly!

ANNA. People will be wondering where he is. People will be *looking* for him. Let's not do this.

JANE. Whose is it?

MARIELLA. Jane.

JANE. Anna, who's the father?

ANNA. *Please.*

> *A fizzing, crackling silence.* ANNA *and* JANE *stare at each other and it's as if by osmosis, how* JANE *realises the truth.*

JANE. No. No, no no. Oh, I am so fucking stupid. You never wanted me to marry him did you?

> *No one moves, no one breathes.*

It was right there the entire time and I didn't, it was all over your face and I just didn't look at it.

MARIELLA. Jane, listen to me –

JANE. Did you know? Did she tell you?

ANNA. She only found out a few days ago. Jane, please, it just – it just happened.

JANE. Did it?

ANNA. I know you don't believe me –

JANE. No, I don't believe you Anna. I've never believed you about anything. How long?

MARIELLA. This isn't important –

JANE. *Shut the fuck up* Mariella! How long?

> ANNA *says nothing.*

I *SAID* HOW FUCKING LONG?!

ANNA. I don't know! Since, since spring.

> JANE *begins to pace, like a boxer in a ring.*

JANE. When in spring? My name day? Before Anne Boleyn was arrested? Before I told you I was betrothed to him?

ANNA. Yes before that, weeks before that.

JANE. So when I told you, when I sat here and *told* you that I was betrothed to him, you just what? You just carried on? Just kept your legs open?

ANNA. I tried to stop it.

JANE. Oh so he forced you?

ANNA. No.

JANE. So he *raped* you?

ANNA. No.

JANE. No because you're not the type of woman who needs to be raped are you Anna?

ANNA. Just cos it wasn't taken by violence doesn't mean it wasn't taken.

JANE *makes a noise, somewhere between a laugh and a snarl.*

JANE. How *poetic* your victimhood is, how beautiful your pillage of my life looks.

ANNA. I'm not trying to be beautiful –

JANE. You are *always* trying to be beautiful, Anna. You fucking sweat with the effort of it! What did he say then? When you told him no, when you told him you didn't want to do it any more, what did he say?

ANNA. I can't remember.

JANE. That's a fucking lie. You remember everything men say to you. It's all you think about. It's all you talk about. It's all you fucking dream about.

ANNA. It was just – it was harder to end it, than I thought.

JANE. Why? Because he was in love with you is that it? Because he couldn't get enough, because Anna is so perfect, Anna is so funny and sharp and rude?

ANNA. That's not what I'm saying –

JANE. Did you even love him? Course you didn't, girl like you doesn't want love, girl like you just wants to *have* something, just wants to be greedy, to have some kind of fucking power –

JANE *SMACKS* ANNA *across the face with such force it makes her stagger back.*

MARIELLA. JANE!

JANE. Does it feel powerful now?!

ANNA *gets to her feet.*

You ruin us all! You ruin us fucking all! *She* has always done this. You have always done this, taking up all the space, sucking up all the air, you have to ruin it, you have to have everything, you can't put up with anything! It's disgusting. I used to pretend like it wasn't but it is and everybody says it. All the men *know*, Anna. Which is why no one will marry you. All of them say yes to your body but no to you. Don't you see that? And I tried to protect you! I tried to *warn* you about what people are saying and and and now look what you've done, look what you did to William.

Hard beat.

ANNA. What?

Silence, the new turn settles in the air between them.
MARIELLA *and* ANNA *stare at* JANE.

JANE. Well, it's true isn't it? You had a weapon in your hand Anna. You picked up a weapon. Why would you pick up a weapon if not to kill him? If not to *try* and kill him?

MARIELLA. She was protecting me.

ANNA. I was protecting Mariella.

JANE. He wasn't even *by* Mariella though, not then.

ANNA. He smacked her.

JANE. He smacked her *once*, just once but you? You wanted to get involved, you wanted to make it about you.

MARIELLA. Jane, don't do this.

JANE. What? I'm just saying what I saw. I'm just saying what she did

ANNA. Richard wanted to fuck me Jane and you're gonna send me to the gallows for it?

JANE. It's not good.

ANNA. Being good isn't important / it's not

JANE. IT *IS* FUCKING IMPORTANT! MY *LIFE*! MY LITTLE LIFE! MY MARRIAGE! MY HUSBAND, MY HOME, MY GOODNESS IS FUCKING IMPORTANT!

ANNA. It was survival.

JANE. Surviving *what*? *Yourself*? You invite destruction like light into a fucking room and look at you! Look at what you have done to me. To that bastard in your fucking belly! To Mariella! Look at William! One house sets alight and it'll turn to ash but if it catches the wind then the whole village goes up in flames and you, Anna, catch the wind every single time – you dance with it, you long for it – and do not care if we *all fucking burn*.

Well, I'm not burning for you.

Beat. MARIELLA *stares hard at* JANE.

ANNA. Fine. Fine. Don't. Don't then.

JANE. Mariella you can stay.

ANNA. We're leaving to protect Mariella.

JANE *looks to* MARIELLA.

JANE. You think she won't cause trouble somewhere else? You think she won't find some new man, who wants to give her diamonds down a fucking alleyway?

ANNA. If you think my guilt will make you innocent, we've not been living in the same England. Mariella, let's go.

ANNA *walks to leave and then realises* MARIELLA *isn't with her.*

Mariella?

MARIELLA *stares at* ANNA, *her chest rising and falling, breath coming in very very fast.*

MARIELLA. She's right.

ANNA. What?

MARIELLA. She's right, Anna, she is, she is, you, you'll find someone, you say you won't, you say we'll go together but and we'll get to London / and there'll be some man

ANNA. No, no no no no / there won't be

MARIELLA. There'll be a man and you, you say you won't but he'll fall in love with you and you'll, you'll go off with / him and I can't

ANNA. Mariella, no / no no no

MARIELLA. And I can't, I, maybe Jane can protect me, maybe Jane can – and William might / understand and and I

ANNA. Mariella look at me, you don't mean this. You're just scared and that's fine because I've been awful, I've been terrible but I promise, if you come with me, I'm going to be better, so please don't do this! Don't fucking do this, don't make me go on my own, please don't do this to me. *Please!* I will be good, I promise, I will be good –

MARIELLA. How can you be when they keep changing what it means?

ANNA. Because I can change! I can change! I will change! I –

But then a noise cuts through and they all freeze – something is coming on the horizon, the sound gets louder, the men get nearer.

MARIELLA. What's that?

They see the men.

JANE. They're coming.

   MARIELLA *turns to* ANNA.

MARIELLA. Run.

   Blackout.

   End of play.

ALMEIDA
THEATRE

The Almeida Theatre makes brave new work that asks big questions: of plays, of theatre and of the world around us. Whether new work or reinvigorated classics, the Almeida brings together the most exciting artists to take risks; to provoke, inspire and surprise our audiences.

Since 2013, the Almeida has been led by Artistic Director Rupert Goold and Executive Director Denise Wood.

Recent highlights include Eline Arbo's Olivier Award-winning adaptation of Nobel Prize-winner Annie Ernaux's *The Years* (transferred to the West End); Jeremy Herrin's production of Sam Holcroft's *A Mirror* (transferred to the West End); Almeida Associate Director Rebecca Frecknall's Olivier Award-winning production *A Streetcar Named Desire* (transferred to the West End and Brooklyn Academy of Music); Rupert Goold's productions of *Tammy Faye* (transferred to Broadway), a new musical from Elton John, Jake Shears and James Graham, and Peter Morgan's *Patriots* (transferred to the West End and Broadway).

Previous productions include Rupert Goold's productions of Steven Sater and Duncan Sheik's *Spring Awakening* (premiered in cinemas UK wide), James Graham's *Ink* (transferred to the West End and Broadway) and Mike Bartlett's *King Charles III* (transferred to West End and Broadway and adapted for BBC television); Rebecca Frecknall's Olivier Award-winning production of Tennessee Williams' *Summer and Smoke* (transferred to West End); Robert Icke's productions of *Hamlet* and *Oresteia* (both of which transferred to New York) and *Mary Stuart* (West End and UK tour); and Lyndsey Turner's Olivier Award-winning production of Lucy Kirkwood's *Chimerica*.

www.nickhernbooks.co.uk

@nickhernbooks